NEW SYSTEMS, METHODS
AND REVELATIONS

Angelika Hoefler

I CHING

NEW SYSTEMS, METHODS AND REVELATIONS

An innovative guide
for all of life's
events and changes

LOTUS LIGHT
SHANGRI-LA

The Author

Angelika Hoefler is a freelance copywriter, who in the course of nearly twenty years of experience has become sensitized against excess, but also towards the essential and meaningful. Among other factors it was her work — frequently taking her backstage of consumerism — that opened her consciousness to an esoterical view of things. She devoted many years to experimentation and research regarding the beyond and reincarnation, including formal studies in applied dianetics and reincarnation therapy.

Herself mediumistically gifted, the author has been engaged in borderline sciences since 1977, activities now of a scope equal to her professional work. Angelika Hoefler is co-creator of what is probably the world's first and only system of reincarnation research using a pendulum.

In the course of her extensive work with various aspects of the karma, the law of cause and effect, she ultimately found new answers to a number of old questions. The results of her research are spectacular methods of cognitive orientation, the ability to determine where one stands at this moment of life, where one belongs and who belongs to one. One of the methods of achieving this has just recently become practicable and is presented in this book for the very first time. In another volume soon to follow, Angelika Hoefler will describe the most important results of her studies of cabbalistic numbers, and also reveal further systems that she has developed.

1. American Edition 1988
by Lotus Light Publications
P.O.Box 2
Wilmot, WI 53192 U.S.A.
The Shangri-La series is published
in cooperation with Schneelöwe Verlagsberatung,
Federal Republic of Germany
Originally published 1988,
© by Schneelöwe Verlagsberatung,
Durach-Bechen, Federal Republic of Germany
All rights reserved
Cover design and illustration: Wolfgang Jünemann
Translation and editing: Peter Hübner
Editorial supervision: Monika Jünemann
Hexagram Art Work: Terry Miller, reprinted with kind permission by Associated Book Publishers (UK) LTD., Hants, England
Production: Schneelöwe, Durach-Bechen, Fed. Rep. of Germany
ISBN 0-9415 24-37-X

Printed 1988 in the Federal Republic of Germany

This book experienced love even before it was completed

The 64 'Faces of Change', represented by the 64 hexagrams that I have attempted to render in words, are accompanied in these pages by drawn meditations created by the British artist Terry Miller, who died 1950 at the age of 31. They were later published as part of the work *Images of Change*. These beautiful picture-interpretations of the Changes of Life now appear here to serve as meditation aids thanks to the efforts of several people posessing two wonderful qualities — they are capable of loving books, and capable of giving friendship. At the time of my work on this book, Monika and Wolfgang Jünemann "discovered" the drawings and were fascinated by their high spiritual content. And last but not least, Miss Alison Hughes in England was happy to give her "Okay".

For that, thank you, with love.

Angelika Hoefler
Cologne, Spring of 1988

Table of Contents

Part I

**I CHING
The key to the Self,
to Your Partner
and to Life Itself**

Introduction

How the I Ching Received Its Name

"Ching" is a Chinese character that translates roughly as "Canonical Book". Canonical in this sense is synonymous with exemplary, in accordance with the canon, which is an old expression for the collection of Biblical books that taught the Faith.

"I" means "chameleon", the lizard that changes its color under conditions such as hunger, fear, temperature fluctuation or varying light. In fact, it behaves very much like a human being, whose aura surrounding and protecting the astral body will show changes of color whenever one's character or state of health undergo a change, or certain emotions are encountered.

The *I Ching — the "Book of Changes"* — is one of the five canonical works that constituted the foundation of philosophical and scientific teaching in the culture of China. This ancient Chinese wisdom was presumably formulated far more than 3000 years ago by King Wen, a forefather of the Chou Dynasty (1122 — 249 B.C.) and preserved in the form of the 64 characters that we today call hexagrams.

The "Book of Changes" — a Book for Your Life

The I Ching is a guide that can offer you directions in every conceivable situation: information, teaching, warning, encouragement or advice, and in every instance no less than the truth.

When you enter into a dialog with the I Ching, your way will become apparent and, at the same time, negotiable for you, however much it may change in the course of time.

Working with the I Ching means letting yourself in for a profound experience: a stranger offers you his or her hand — and in that very moment you know that this is a friend, but also that you are facing a mirror.

64 Hexagrams — the "DNA of the Spirit"?

There is one unquestionable proof of the universality and all encompassing applicability of the I Ching: our lives themselves; the number 64.

The I Ching contains 64 hexagrams or separate informations. Human experience is made up of 64 archetypal situations. 64 triplets regulate the genetic code.

The 64 hexagrams are faithful copies of the 64 triplets that control the amino acids in DNA, the carrier of our genetic blueprint, and thereby insure conformity with the energetical laws that govern all present life.

And just as each triplet, each triune entity, works united to maintain the cosmic order of mankind, so the three-line trigrams, of which two equal a six-line hexagram, are available to every human being to help him or her maintain or re-establish the cosmic order of the spirit.

Answers From Inside?

This consideration is utterly bold, and yet temptingly scientific and almost obvious at the same time, qualities that in most cases tend to contradict each other:

Perhaps those triplets connect us "from the inside out" (the same way the genetic code is read) with certain trigrams that are meant for us and with which we construct the hexagram, and thereby — and perhaps therefore — receive the correct answer to our question.

That would also solve the puzzle of coincidence and disprove the validity of accidental occurrance for a new reason.

Coincidence is when two necessary events can reliably be counted on to occur simultaneously and in conjunction with each other. In this case, for example, the question and the answer in a sense become each other's honest and reliable partner within the I Ching.

The I Ching always provides the right answer, when it is consulted seriously and reasonably. For all who trust it, the mystical mask is laid aside and it presents itself as a friend. And it would be difficult indeed to find someone who has given up a friendship with the I Ching, unless he or she could not bear the truth.

For your friendship with the I Ching I wish you courage and a sense of humor; sometimes one really does need both.

Foreword

First of all, I would like to explain something:

In order to enhance a system of 'essential information' that will be welcomed especially by all newcomers to the I Ching, I have omitted the classic transformations, the Lines of Change, that every other book on I Ching that I know of contains, but I have included the changes themselves.

So if you would like to study the very involved structure of the I Ching or additionally consult the Lines of Change, a number of excellent works on the subject are available, the best of which have been translated directly from the Chinese by truly knowledgeable experts. So much for that, because I certainly don't want to suggest that you should be reading every other book on the subject except this one.

Based on the I Ching I will demonstrate the results of my own years of intensive research with the I Ching and the Cabbala of Numbers, which will be discussed further later on.

With this book I present you heretofore unknown systems from the realm of 'borderline science' that in certain life situations will assist you in reaching solid basic cognition, in other words, the recognition of the essential that can lead to determining proper action.

Abilities Gained Through This Book

As life aspects we differentiate between two key circumstances in life: that which rules *now* = *the changing situation* (also the result of things past and the cause of things future), and that which rules *generally* = *the static situation*. Each situation is treated in a separate section of the book.

Part II is a course in cognition orientation. It will enable you to determine the general and therefore static or merely minutely changing situation and with it the constellation of people, events and day-dates, so that you will be able to avoid mistakes and be guarded against possible unpleasant experiences.

Part III is an adviser. It will make you familiar with the Now, the situation subject to change. The 64 hexagrams contain guidelines for all of life's events and changes, so that you will be able to appraise yourself, others, a given circumstance, your work situation or a relationship with certainty, and reach a considered decision.

Life Aspect:
Now as a Changing Situation

Asking the I Ching about the Now-Situation

You can consult the I Ching in two possible situations:

a) When you want to know what constitutes NOW, what (fluctuating) circumstances rule at the time of your asking. Here we employ the "coin method" described further on.

b) When you want to know what rules GENERALLY, which (static) situations you have to deal with. Here we employ the system of Cognition Orientation described in detail in *Part II*.

The interpretations of the hexagrams are designed so that they can be read for both situations according to the following scheme:

1. *The Person*
   Psychological characteristics
   a) at the time of asking
   b) generally

2. *The Situation*
   Perspectives of a case in point
   a) at the time of asking
   b) generally

3. *Partnership*
   Situation analysis and action guide-lines
   a) for the time of asking
   b) generally

4. *Advice*
   Tactics
   a) relative to the information gained
   b) generally

The "Coin Method"

The method is simple, but not without considerable effect. Take three identical coins and hold them in your cupped hands.

Concentrate on your question. Keep your mind on the question as you shake the coins in your hands. Then throw them.

Each throw determines one line of a hexagram to be drawn.

You score: "Heads" = 2, a broken line   __ __
            "Tails" = 3, an unbroken line _____

Possible results could look like this:

2 + 2 + 2 = 6 = even = __ __ (broken line)
3 + 3 + 3 = 9 = odd = _____ (unbroken line)
2 + 2 + 3 = 7 = odd = _____ (unbroken line)
3 + 3 + 2 = 8 = even = __ __ (broken line)

In order to create a hexagram, you require six lines *(hexa* is a Greek prefix meaning *six).*

Note: A hexagram is always constructed *from bottom to top.* In a sense the answer grows, as our understanding of correlations must grow.

The key to the hexagrams that will let you find the one you are looking for is readily found at the end of the book.

Life Aspect:
The Static or Minutely
Changing Situation

The Symbiosis of I Ching and Cabbala

The I Ching being the Book of Changes, it appears natural that consulting it can illuminate situations (by the "Coin Method", for example) that are in a process of change and transformation. But obviously a counterpoint is required in order to recognize static or minutely changing situations, a cognitive key that takes into account the ruling criterion of consistency as well as the influencing criterion of latent change. This therefore has to be an element somehow related to the I Ching.

I discovered it in the Cabbala of Numbers, which I have been researching in depth since 1977, and have since expanded by a two-digit number of cognitive systems, which is, however, not meant to be the theme of this book.

The Cabbala of Numbers makes it possible to define the meanings of names, concepts, dates, events etc., because a person's name is not simply a personal or social means of identification. It is just as much a transcendental code of his genetic make-up, his karma and, in combination with his date of birth, a key to his way in life, his trials, but also his opportunities and goals. The basis for working with the Cabbala of Numbers is a 'Cabbalistic Code' that makes it possible to transform the letters of a name or any concept into numbers, which are then transformed into information again.

Part II

Cognition Orientation —
I Ching and Cabbala
as Components of the
Symbiosis for Recognition

Introduction to Cognition Orientation

Working with the two components of Cognition Orientation, the I Ching and the Cabbala of Numbers, is by no means a privilege of the precognitively gifted or of acknowledged sensitives. Instead, it opens the door for anyone seeking truth and perception. I have chosen *cognition* as the keystone term, because cognito is the Latin word for 'gaining knowledge', getting to know something well.

The second method of consulting the I Ching, published here for the first time, was conceived primarily to enhance cognition — *re-cognition* — and only secondarily for the purpose of gaining advice and guidance.

When you work with *Part II*, you will receive information that applies to *static or only minutely changing situations*, existing facts that only people undergoing changes themselves are able to modify to a certain degree (given that no karmic reasons related to destiny prevent this).

Introducing the Cognitograms

On the basis of the hexagrams shown in *Part III* you can now construct the following Cognitograms, i.e. concepts of recognition:

1. The Person

A. *Personality Hexagram*
You gain information about your own character traits or those of another person.

Possible questions: What should I know in order to understand a certain person better? What are his or her strengths and weaknesses?

B. *Career Hexagram*
Using an established professional designation or title (for ex-

ample lawyer, accountant or technician) as a basis, you can determine how well someone is suited for his or her occupation.

Possible questions: What are my chances of success or advancement in a given profession? What about other lines of business? What difficulties might have to be expected?

2. The Situation

A. *Event Hexagram*

You can receive a day's prognosis for any date you choose, provided you know the birthday of the person in question.

Possible questions: How will a certain day turn out for me (or another person)? How will a sporting event end? Which horse should I bet on? What may I expect from an introductory interview, a business date, a court hearing? What will be the consequences if I begin a trip, sign a lease, buy a car, a house, a yacht etc. on a certain day?

B. *Influence Hexagram*

In the same manner in which we can determine a person's suitability for a given occupation or gauge our harmony with a certain partner, we can also find out in other situations, what factors are influencing us or another person, and how.

Possible questions: What influences await me at a new personal or business address? What kind of an impression does a given company or product name make on the public? Which book or film title is most apt to be successful? Which influences am I under in a certain place?

3. Partnership

Compatibility Hexagram

This hexagram reveals how two people regard each other, and thereby, whether or not they are suited for partnership (personal or business) with each other.

Possible questions: How am I being appraised by my steady date, superior, employee, colleague, neighbor or relative?

How does my subconscious rate that particular person? How do we harmonize? What are the consequences if I enter into a contract of any sort with a certain person?

The Secret of the 22

Comprehension of the method of cognition developed by me (without a doubt in co-operation with kindred spirits), which may in fact be a "rediscovery", will be easier if the following is remembered:

The Cabbala of Numbers is, in a sense, a newer branch of the ancient tree of the Jewish "Kabbalah", and it, too, uses the base of 22 sacred numbers that are identical with the letter sequence of the Hebrew alphabet. In a doubly interesting way they can be traced back to the solar alphabet also consisting of 22 letters, whose roots reach back far more than 5000 years to the morphological Vattan-alphabet:

Contrary to the lunar, moon-oriented spirit the solar, sun-oriented frame of spirit is traditionally recognized as self-knowledge.

This lets us sense that the 22 Letters of the solar alphabet, carried on in the Hebrew tradition, contain an unimaginable store of coded knowledge.

As we continue researching the roots of the Cabbala of Numbers we are confronted by a species in the Vattan-alphabet, that was written from the bottom up, exactly the way the hexagrams of the I Ching were constructed.

The constellation of these insights suggests the practically inevitable conclusion that a symbiosis of I Ching and Cabbala must be the double key to the door of knowledge.

I have tried it; it fits.

I hereby place it in your hand.

The Cabbalistic Code

Where with the coin method "heads" or "tails" are the basis for constructing individual hexagram-lines, the make-up of a Cognitogram uses the cabbalistic number equivalents of a name or a term (see alphabet-key) or, if applicable, the numbers of a certain date (see date-key).

International Alphabet-Key			
a, ä	1	a, ä	1
b	2	b	2
g	3	c	11
d	4	d	4
e	5	e	5
u, ü, v, w	6	f	17
z	7	g	3
h, ch	8	h, ch	8
t	9	i, j	10
i, j, y	10	k	11
c, k	11	l	12
l	12	m	13
m	13	n	14
n	14	o, ö	16
x	15	p, ph	17
o, ö	16	q	19
f, p, ph	17	r	20
sch, sh, ts, tz	18	s	21
q	19	sch, sh	18
r	20	t	9
s	21	th	22
th	22	ts, tz	18
		u, ü, v, w	6
		x	15
		y	10
		z	7

a) When calculating, it is important to have in mind that the letter combinations *ch, ph, sch, sh, th, ts* and *tz* are always scored as one unit with the values shown.
(Example: sch is 18, *not* s [21], c [11], and h [8], which would equal 40!).

b) **Cross-adding the digits**
In order to arrive at a hexagram-line the result arrived at according to the alphabet-key, usually consisting of two digits, is reduced to a one-digit figure by adding the given numbers in sequence left to right horizontally.

Example: The total arrived at is 48.
$$48 = 4 + 8 = 12 = 1 + 2 = 3$$

c) **Date-key**

Date								
1	2	3	4	5	6	7	8	9
10	11	12	13	14	15	16	17	18
19	20	21	22	23	24	25	26	27
28	29	30	31					
equals								
1	2	3	4	5	6	7	8	9

d) **Multiple-digit results are reduced to one figure.**
In the construction of a Cognitogram *one-digit figures* only are used. If necessary, multiple-digit dates (day, month or year) are reduced to one digit by repeated cross-addition, as described under c) (above).

e) **Mathematical steps**
1. In the case of names and other concepts the corresponding numbers for *vowels* have to be added *first* and, if necessary, reduced to one digit by cross-addition. Where you are working with personal names, calculate the given and family names and, if applicable, designations of nobility (of, van, von, de). Do not, however, include academic titles (M.A., Dr., Prof.).

Note: If the result of the calculation is a one-digit even number, a broken line expressing the female principle YIN is made = __ __.

Should the result be a one-digit odd number, an unbroken line expressing the male principle YANG is made = _____.

2. Secondly, the consonants are calculated as described previously.

3. The *third line* is the one-digit result of the cross-addition of all additions made.
   Example:

Sum of vowels	45
Sum of consonants	42
Sum total:	87

   Cross-adding 87 = 8 + 7 = 15 (two-digit)
   Cross-adding 15 = 1 + 5 = 6 (one-digit)
   = broken line = __ __.

4. When calculating dates, *first* determine the one-digit day number that also results in a broken line when it is even and an unbroken line when it is an odd number. (Example: a day date of 24 is calculated 2 + 4 = 6 = a broken line = __ __).

5. *Secondly,* the month figure is determined. (The months October, November and December are reduced to their one-digit numbers: 10 = 1, 11 = 2, 12 = 3).

6. The third date-line (= the sixth and uppermost line of the hexagram) is the cross-added sum of the year number. (The year 1900 is calculated: 1 + 9 = 10, 1 + 0 = 1 = an unbroken line. The year 1999: 1 + 9 + 9 + 9 = 28 = 2 + 8 = 10 = 1 + 0 = 1 = also an unbroken line).

Rule

The lines of a Cognitogram (whether trigram or hexagram) are *always* built up from bottom to top.

In the case of Cognitograms consisting of names and dates (Personality Hexagrams, Event Hexagrams, possibly Influence Hexagrams), the name trigram is below and the number trigram above. (For Cognitograms constructed of two names or terms, see Compatibility Hexagrams; for those consisting of two dates, see daily trigrams).

Example of a Cognitogram

The figures shown under paragraphs 1 to 6 would be added to create the following hexagram:

Below: the Name Trigram.

Vowels: $45 = 4 + 5 = \quad 9 =$ the unbroken first line.
Consonants: $42 = 4 + 2 = \quad 6 =$ the broken second line.
Sum total: $\overline{87} = 8 + 7 = 15 =$
                      $1 + 5 = \quad 6 =$ the broken third line.

Above: the Number Trigram using the 24th of December, 1900.

Day 24: $24 = 2 + 4 = \quad 6 =$ the broken fourth line.
Month 12: $12 = 1 + 2 = \quad 3 =$ the unbroken fifth line.
Year 1900: $19 = 1 + 9 = 10 =$
                    $10 = 1 + 0 = \quad 1 =$ the unbroken sixth line.

Result:

HEXAGRAM 42 — MULTIPLICATION: ───── 6
                                                      ───── 5
                                                      ── ── 4
                                                      ── ── 3
                                                      ── ── 2
                                                      ───── 1

The Trigrams

The trigram can be viewed as "the one half of cognition" because a hexagram consists of two trigrams placed one above the other.

Every trigram has an affinity to special attributes: to one of the eight archetypal family members, an aspect of nature, a color, a part of the body, an animal, a form of energy, a season, a direction, and a time of day, given here approximately. Beyond that, each trigram represents certain qualities, the most important of which are listed at the end of this chapter.

Once we know these traditional qualities or analogies, each trigram becomes a valuable source of parts of information that can be employed advantageously in cases where a date necessary for the construction of a hexagram may not be known, or we are interested in simply finding out the significance of a word, the quality of a concept, of a certain thing or process.

Additionally, the trigram gives us valuable supplementary information regarding the hexagram we have arrived at, even the "whys" of a certain character, a situation or a partnership.

Trigram Analogies*

Times shown using the international 24 hour scale
(11 PM = 23.00, 9.15 PM = 21.15, etc.).

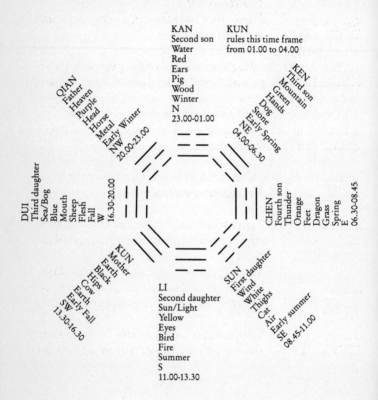

KAN
Second son
Water
Red
Ears
Pig
Wood
Winter
N
23.00-01.00

KUN
rules this time frame
from 01.00 to 04.00

KEN
Third son
Mountain
Green
Hands
Dog
Stone
Early Spring
NE
04.00-06.30

QIAN
Father
Heaven
Purple
Head
Horse
Metal
Early Winter
NW
20.00-23.00

DUI
Third daughter
Sea/Bog
Blue
Mouth
Sheep
Flesh
Fall
W
16.30-20.00

CHEN
Fourth son
Thunder
Orange
Feet
Dragon
Grass
Spring
E
06.30-08.45

KUN
Mother
Earth
Black
Hips
Cow
Earth
Early Fall
SW
13.30-16.30

LI
Second daughter
Sun/Light
Yellow
Eyes
Bird
Fire
Summer
S
11.00-13.30

SUN
First daughter
Wind
White
Thighs
Cat
Air
Early summer
SE
08.45-11.00

---

* Circular depiction of the trigrams according to King Wen.

Qualities of the Trigrams

≡ QIAN — The giving; creativity; power; inspiration; energy; brightness; completeness; agressiveness; coldness; sound; word; might.

☷ KUN — The receiving; kindness; protection; equanimity; weakness; yielding; darkness; warmth; lastingness.

☳ CHEN — Influence; impulsiveness; provocation; potency; concussion; experiment; creativity.

☴ SUN — Gentility; pervasion; ease, lightness; keensightedness; movement; formality; fleetingness.

☵ KAN — Danger; work; flexibility; melancholy; abysses; fear; control; prejudices.

☲ LI — Enlightenment; clarity; intelligence; warmth; communication; togetherness; dependency.

☶ KEN — Modesty; conscientiousness; immobility; reliability; faithfulness; unalterability. In the metaphysical sense: beginning and end.

☱ DUI — Contentment; amusement; magic; destruction; openness; excess; naiveness; liveliness.

The System of a Trigram

In accordance with the Cabbalistic Code and the previously established rule of number reduction, let us first of all construct trigrams for the two main aspects of this book, the I Ching and the Cabbala, and examine their meaning as well as their probably ancient relationship to each other.

Example: The trigram for "I Ching"

1. The numbers equivalent of the *vowels* contained in the name "I Ching" serve to determine the first or bottom line:
   $I(10) + i(10) = 20 = 2 =$ __ __

2. The numbers equivalent of the *consonants* in "I Ching" determine the second line:
   $Ch(8) + n(14) + g(3) = 25 = 7 =$ _____

3. The numbers equivalent of *all of the letters* in "I Ching" determine the third line:
   $I(10) + Ch(8) + i(10) + n(14) + g(3) = 45 = 9 =$ _____

The resulting trigram: _____ 3.
                            _____ 2. = SUN
                            __ __ 1.

It is the trigram with the Chinese designation SUN, having, among others, the attributes of keensightedness and pervasion.

Example: The trigram for "Cabbala"

1. Using the number equivalents of the *vowels* contained in the word "Cabbala", the first line is determined:
   $a(1) + a(1) + a(1) = 3 =$ _____

2. Using the number equivalents of the *consonants* contained in the word "Cabbala", the second line is determined:
   $C(11) + b(2) + b(2) + l(12) = 27 = 9 =$ _____

3. Using the number equivalents of all of the letters contained in "Cabbala", the third line is determined:
   $C(11) + a(1) + b(2) + b(2) + a(1) + l(12) + a(1) = 30$
   $= 3 =$ _____

The resulting trigram: _____ 3.
                       _____ 2. = QIAN
                       _____ 1.

We are dealing with the trigram QIAN, which has the qualities father, heaven and the creative attributed to it (see previous trigram analogies and attributes).

Trigram Cognition

A. National Meanings

Every name and every concept represents information. For instance, when we examine the origin of names we find historical regions, cities, rivers and places of special geographic interest. We also find attributes, possessions, trades and much more.

Etymology, the science of language origin and development, teaches us a great deal about the multibranched roots that words have, about the meaning they once had and their transition into modern times. We can see that every word is a representative of its time — because vocabularies change, too —, every word characterizes the feeling of the people that lived in a given time, or perhaps regarding a certain event. In the same sense dialects testify to a very specific relationship people had or have to a word. Apparently, attitudes are varied when different people refer to the same thing using different terms, just as there is an 'indigenous understanding' when slang is spoken in typical daily use, or in the terminology used by various professionals and other specialists (consider, for example, the trade encyclopedia used by doctors and computer specialists).

So we see that language can simultaneously reveal and conceal things. The German philosopher, theologian and poet Johann Gottfried von Herder summed it up with the words: "Language is reflection."

Therefore now a few national and slightly international examples of word trigrams to reflect upon:

In these examples of trigrams constructed according to the Cabbalistic Code, V stands for *vowels*, C for *consonants* and T for *total*.

GOD
1. V   16 = 7   3. _____ QIAN.
2. C   7 = 7   2. _____ The giving;
3. T   23 = 5   1. _____ father; heaven;
                                completeness.

NATURE
1. V   12 = 3   3. _____ QIAN.
2. C   43 = 7   2. _____ The creative;
3. T   55 = 10 = 1   1. _____ power;
                                energy.

SPIRIT
1. V   20 = 2   3. __ __ KUN.
2. C   67 = 13 = 4   2. __ __ The receiving;
3. T   87 = 15 = 6   1. __ __ kindness;
                              lastingness.

SPIRITUALITY
1. V   37 = 10 = 1   3. _____ LI.
2. C   98 = 17 = 8   2. __ __ Enlightenment;
3. T   135 = 9   1. _____ clarity;
                                togetherness;
                                communication;
                                warmth.

MATTER
1. V   6 = 6   3. _____ KEN.
2. C   51 = 6   2. __ __ Conscien-
3. T   57 = 12 = 3   1. __ __ tiousness; im-
                              mobility;
                              metaphysically:
                              beginning and
                              end.

KARMA	1. V 2 = 2	3. _____ KEN.
	2. C 44 = 8	2. __ __ Unalterability;
	3. T 46 = 10 = 1	1. __ __ metaphysically: beginning and end.

DEATH	1. V 6 = 6	3. _____ KEN.
	2. C 26 = 8	2. __ __ Unalterability;
	3. T 32 = 5	1. __ __ metaphysically: beginning and end.

REINCAR- NATION	1. V 43 = 7	3. _____ QIAN Power;
	2. C 102 = 3	2. _____ brightness;
	3. T 145 = 10 = 1	1. _____ aggressiveness; might; word.

B. International meanings

In principle all one needs to do is to open the Bible and immerse oneself in a fascinating study of names in order to gain certain elemental insights, because biblical names are codes, and this at least is no mystery. And since they are the same the world over, they can theoretically transmit the same information and insights to all people. This principle is so old that we no longer take note of it in daily life, and yet we meet with it everywhere.

Why are names and concepts of worldwide interest to the public internationalized? Is it so that we all pronounce them in the same manner? That could be one possibility. But why then are personal names never translated?

Words, concepts, terms and names are information posessing a particular vibration. If a word is translated, its information vibration is altered, and so are the emotions that it can activate.

If one were to translate a personal name, that would be an attempt to alter a person. People do, however, change their names themselves and thereby assume vibrations of a different quality, enter a new field of resonance and into a new frame of experience.

Therefore the international spelling of a name or a concept assures a uniform international "reflection". Ancient and current history is full of examples of this. Here is a selection of "international trigrams" that illustrate the point and hopefully serve as a stimulus for personal study.

Trigram	Name/Term/Concept	Qualities
QIAN	Dalai Lama	The giving; creativity; power; brightness; inspiration.
	Mandala	Inspiration; power; brightness.
	WHO (World Health Organisation)	Energy; brightness; completeness; power.
	UNESCO	The giving; creativity; inspiration; brightness; completeness.
KUN	Golden Gate Bridge	Equanimity; protection; lastingness.
CHEN	Aristotle	Influence; creativity; inspiration; power.
	OM (sacred mantra)	Influence.
SUN	Socrates	Pervasion; keensightedness.
KAN	NATO	Work; flexibility; control.
LI	Ra (Egyptian sun god)	Enlightenment; warmth.

	UNICEF	Togetherness; communication; warmth.
	Greenpeace	Togetherness; communication; intelligence.
KEN	Yoga	Modesty; immobility; faithfulness; metaphysically: beginning and end.
	Amnesty International	Conscientiousness; reliability; metaphysically: beginning and end.
DUI	Titanic	Excess; destruction.

C. Comparing national and international meanings

Identical meaning in the languages of various countries has far-reaching historical roots that did not in all cases lead to a sameness of character traits, but do represent a common origin of identical interpretation.

Speaking in trigrams, the word "God" means "Father, heaven, Creation" in Anglo-Saxon usage, and is represented by the trigram QIAN. The same applies to the term "nature". Different people literally speak the same language, in these cases the Anglo-Saxons and the German-speaking populations of Germany, Switzerland and Austria.

How, specifically, people in various countries regard a particular matter and feel about it, depends on their genetic heritage, their upbringing and social environment, their customs, traditions and their own language. The mentality-scale that becomes discernable in Trigram Cognition can be used by us to build a bridge of understanding. We can learn to understand better what goes on in the hearts and minds of people who speak a different language, and perhaps then it won't be quite as difficult to find the "right words" for each other.

A few examples of English and German terms in comparison may help to illustrate this:

SPIRIT = KUN
The receiving; kindness; lastingness.

GEIST = KEN
Conscientiousness; reliability; metaphysically: beginning and end.

SPIRITUALITY = LI
Enlightenment; clarity; communication; formality. warmth.

SPIRITUALITÄT = SUN
Pervasion; keensightedness; togetherness;

MATTER = KEN
Conscientiousness; immobility; togetherness.

MATERIE = LI
Intelligence; communication; metaphysically: beginning and end.

KARMA = KEN
Unalterability; metaphysically: beginning and end.

KARMA = KEN
(Same association as in English, as this is a Sanskrit term that cannot be translated. Karma is the concept of the cosmic law of cause and effect).

DEATH = KEN
Unalterability; metaphysically: beginning and end.

TOD = KEN
(Same association as in English, although this is by far not the case in all languages. Interesting in this context is, that the Latin "mors" leads us to the trigram QIAN and therewith to the old meaning of the word death: "The giving; power; energy; brightness", as

opposed to "aggressiveness; coldness.").

REINCARNATION = QIAN
Power; brightness; aggressiveness; might; word.

REINKARNATION = QIAN
(Same association as in English. Examining the differences of associations in Anglo-Saxon and German terms regarding the concepts "Spirit/Geist" and "Spirituality/Spiritualität" clarifies why spirituality is more strongly emphasized in the United States and England than it is in German-speaking countries).

The Meanings of the 64 Hexagrams*

<table>
<tr><td>1</td><td>The Creative Power</td><td>33</td><td>The Withdrawal</td></tr>
<tr><td>2</td><td>The Receiving</td><td>34</td><td>The Great Might</td></tr>
<tr><td>3</td><td>Difficulty starting</td><td>35</td><td>Progress</td></tr>
<tr><td>4</td><td>Inexperience</td><td>36</td><td>Eclipse of Light</td></tr>
<tr><td>5</td><td>Considered Waiting</td><td>37</td><td>The Family</td></tr>
<tr><td>6</td><td>The Conflict</td><td>38</td><td>The Opposite</td></tr>
<tr><td>7</td><td>Gathered Strength</td><td>39</td><td>The Blockade</td></tr>
<tr><td>8</td><td>Union</td><td>40</td><td>The Liberation</td></tr>
<tr><td>9</td><td>The Hindrance</td><td>41</td><td>Reduction</td></tr>
<tr><td>10</td><td>Behavior</td><td>42</td><td>Multiplication</td></tr>
<tr><td>11</td><td>Prospering</td><td>43</td><td>The Breakthrough</td></tr>
<tr><td>12</td><td>The Standstill</td><td>44</td><td>The Meeting</td></tr>
<tr><td>13</td><td>Togetherness</td><td>45</td><td>The Collection</td></tr>
<tr><td>14</td><td>Prosperity</td><td>46</td><td>The Ascent</td></tr>
<tr><td>15</td><td>Moderation</td><td>47</td><td>Distress</td></tr>
<tr><td>16</td><td>Enthusiasm</td><td>48</td><td>The Well</td></tr>
<tr><td>17</td><td>The Succession</td><td>49</td><td>The Upheaval</td></tr>
<tr><td>18</td><td>The Restoration</td><td>50</td><td>The Cosmic Order</td></tr>
<tr><td>19</td><td>The Nearing</td><td>51</td><td>Thunder</td></tr>
<tr><td>20</td><td>Observation</td><td>52</td><td>The Silence</td></tr>
<tr><td>21</td><td>Prevailing Against Odds</td><td>53</td><td>Development</td></tr>
<tr><td>22</td><td>Loveliness</td><td>54</td><td>Propriety</td></tr>
<tr><td>23</td><td>Deterioration</td><td>55</td><td>Abundance</td></tr>
<tr><td>24</td><td>The New Beginning</td><td>56</td><td>The Traveller</td></tr>
<tr><td>25</td><td>The Unexpected</td><td>57</td><td>Pervasion</td></tr>
<tr><td>26</td><td>The Great Taming Power</td><td>58</td><td>Joy</td></tr>
<tr><td>27</td><td>Nourishment</td><td>59</td><td>Dissolution</td></tr>
<tr><td>28</td><td>Excess</td><td>60</td><td>The Limitation</td></tr>
<tr><td>29</td><td>Danger</td><td>61</td><td>Insight</td></tr>
<tr><td>30</td><td>The Fire</td><td>62</td><td>The Moderate Excess</td></tr>
<tr><td>31</td><td>The Attraction</td><td>63</td><td>After Completion</td></tr>
<tr><td>32</td><td>The Duration</td><td>64</td><td>Prior to Completion</td></tr>
</table>

---

*The names of the 64 hexagrams are based on a multitude of translations of Chinese writings, which in many cases differentiate only minutely from each other. The most frequently found translations are the ones used in this book.

Hexagram Cognition

1. The Person

A. The System of Personality Hexagrams

A Personality Hexagram is constructed using the two components of the given name and family name (= lower trigram) and the date of birth (= upper trigram).

The publicly common name is used, and if someone has more than one given name, the one by which he or she is called. Where applicable, stage or pen names are used, but not academic titles.*

---

*Historical personalities are calculated with their complete historical names in their own language. For this reason the Roman numerals often following their names have to written out in full.
Examples:

George III	George The Third, Wilhelm Friedrich, born June 6, 1738, Personality Hexagram 4: Inexperience.
Elisabeth II	Elisabeth The Second, born April 21, 1926, Personality Hexagram 50: The Cosmic Order.
Diana, Princess of Wales	Diana, Princess of Wales, born July 1, 1961, Personality Hexagram 47: Distress.
Charles, Prince of Wales	Charles, Prince of Wales, born November 14, 1948, Personality Hexagram 25: The Unexpected.
Louis XVI	Louis Seize, born August 23, 1754, Personality Hexagram 35: The Great Might.
Peter (I) the Great, Czar and Emperor of Russia	Piotr I. Aleksejevitch, born June 9, 1672, Personality Hexagram 64: Prior to Completion.
Elisabeth, Empress of Austria, Queen of Hungary	Elisabeth, born December 24, 1837, Personality Hexagram 61: The Insight.

Examples Showing Addition and Interpretation

Personality Hexagram of JOHANN WOLFGANG VON GOETHE, born August 28, 1749.

The designation of nobility will not be used here, an exception for a reason that will be explained and justified at the end.

The Personality Hexagram of Johann Wolfgang Goethe reads as follows:

JOHANN WOLFGANG GOETHE

	V 60 = 6	_____	
	C 126 = 9	__ __	
	T 186 = 15 = 6	_____	64: Prior to
Day of birth: 28	28 = 10 = 1	__ __	Completion
Month of birth: 8	8 = 8 = 8	_____	
Year of birth: 1749	21 = 3 = 3	__ __	

Now read hexagram 64 and you will probably be surprised to learn that Goethe apparently needed "beginner's luck", which may not coincide with your previous impression of the famous Privy Councillor.

And yet this is correct. Since Goethe was born of common lineage and only later in life achieved nobility, I have chosen this example to also illustrate personal development activated by a change of name.

If using "von" Goethe, the following Personality Hexagram results:

JOHANN WOLFGANG *VON* GOETHE

V 76 = 13 = 4	_____	
C 146 = 11 = 2	__ __	
T 222 = 6 = 6	_____	35:
28 = 10 = 1	__ __	Progress
8 = 8 = 8	__ __	
21 = 3 = 3	__ __	

Now read hexagram 35 and you will see that Johann Wolfgang von Goethe was practically predestined to achieve greatness one day.

Personality Hexagrams of Famous Persons

You can look up the hexagram corresponding to the number shown for personalities that interest you.

Name	Date of birth (day, month, year)	Hexagram
Tomaso Albinoni	8. 6. 1671	24
Louis Armstrong	4. 7. 1900	59
Neil Armstrong	5. 8. 1930	34
Joan Baez	9. 1. 1941	17
Simone de Beauvoir	9. 1. 1908	33
Leonard Bernstein	25. 8. 1918	56
Joseph Beuys	12. 5. 1921	43
Heinrich Böll	21. 12. 1917	13
Humphrey Bogart	25. 12. 1899	10
Wilhelm Busch	15. 4. 1832	27
Marcus Tullius Cicero	3. 1. 106 B.C.	12
Salvador Dali	11. 5. 1904	57
Erich von Däniken	14. 4. 1935	50
Erich Däniken (minus "von")	14. 4. 1935	56
Bette Davis	5. 4. 1908	30
James Dean	8. 2. 1931	27
Albert Einstein	14. 3. 1879	25
Anne Frank	12. 6. 1929	14
Benjamin Franklin	17. 1. 1706	42
Sigmund Freud	6. 5. 1856	3
Indira Gandhi	19. 11. 1917	30
Johann Wolfgang von Goethe	28. 8. 1749	35
Edvard Grieg	15. 6. 1843	22
Hermann Hesse	2. 7. 1877	37

Alfred Hitchcock	13. 8. 1899	41
Carl Gustav Jung	26. 7. 1875	61
Franz Kafka	3. 7. 1883	43
Buster Keaton	4. 10. 1896	29
John F. Kennedy	29. 5. 1917	59
Martin Luther King	15. 1. 1929	61
John Lennon	9. 10. 1940	10
Martin Luther	10. 11. 1483	35
Rosa Luxemburg	5. 3. 1870	1
Mao Tse Tung	26. 12. 1893	61
Somerset Maugham	25. 1. 1874	17
Alexander Mitscherlich	20. 9. 1908	61
Marilyn Monroe	1. 6. 1926	21
Wolfgang Amadeus Mozart	27. 1. 1756	44
Florence Nightingale	12. 5. 1820	49
Anaïs Nin	21. 2. 1903	40
Nostradamus		
(Michel de Notre Dame)	14. 10. 1503	44
Jacques Offenbach	20. 6. 1819	22
Edgar Allan Poe	19. 1. 1809	44
Elvis Presley	8. 1. 1935	37
Anthony Quinn	21. 4. 1915	56
Ronald Reagan	6. 2. 1911	52
Maximilien Robespierre	6. 5. 1758	9
Jean Paul Sartre	21. 6. 1905	55
Frank Sinatra	12. 12. 1915	6
Helmut Schmidt	3. 12. 1918	10
Edith Stein	12. 10. 1891	1
John Steinbeck	27. 2. 1902	14
Elizabeth Taylor	27. 2. 1932	16
Margaret Thatcher	13. 10. 1925	29
Liv Ullmann	16. 12. 1938	13
Amerigo Vespucci	9. 3. 1451	47
Richard Wagner	22. 5. 1813	29
George Washington	22. 2. 1732	7
Tennessee Williams	26. 3. 1911	42

Richard von Weizsäcker   15. 4. 1920   22
Karol Wojtyla (John Paul II)   18. 5. 1920   1
William Butler Yeats   13. 6. 1865   2

B. The System of the Career Hexagram

The Career Hexagram is made up of the two components of the given and family name (= lower trigram) and professional title (= upper trigram).

The paragraphs on hexagrams entitled "The Person" and "The Situation" should then be consulted. The paragraph "Advice" may be additionally helpful. All of the rules mentioned under A. (previous) apply here also.

Note: If you are constructing a Career Hexagram for someone who was born or lives in a different language area, the professional title must be given in the applicable language (see also "Trigram Cognition", A. — C.).

In the following examples this rule has been applied, for the interested reader the original designations are shown in parenthesis.

Examples Showing Addition and Interpretation

Career Hexagram of JOHANN WOLFGANG VON GOETHE.
Before Goethe discovered literature as the fulfillment of his life, he successfully studied Law, which he practised for a few years in Frankfurt.

His Career Hexagram consists of the previously constructed (lower) Name Trigram

$$\equiv\equiv \text{ KUN}$$

and the Career Trigram (the professional title) placed above it.

JURIST	(Jurist)	V 16	= 7	
		C 60	= 6	$\equiv\equiv$ CHEN
		T 76	= 13 = 4	

41

And combined they look like this:

≡≡ 16:
≡≡ En-
——— thusi-
asm

The hexagram rubric "The Person" already begins to reveal that Goethe exercised this profession less like an analytical thinker and more like a 'person of feeling', and remained in it most likely due to a passing infatuation with a career in law. "The Situation" states it clearly: He sought new realms to conquer. How true an analysis. Goethe turned poet, romancier and playwright.

His Career Hexagram as a writer now appears as follows: Name Trigram + Career Trigram "poet" *(Dichter)*.

KUN ≡≡ + ≡≡ KAN   ≡≡ 8:
                                    ≡≡ Unity

The two rubrics that should be consulted here, too, "The Person" and "The Situation", show clearly, that Goethe had immersed himself in an extraordinary life situation and very great responsibility.

Career Hexagrams of Famous Persons

Elisabeth The Second, *Queen, Career Hexagram 32.*
With the Personality Hexagram 50, The Cosmic Order, the Queen of England represents positive energy and charisma, and has lasting influence on people in an ethical as well as an intellectual sense. Hers is a truly majestic depiction of personality that is perfectly augmented by Career Hexagram 32: Faithfulness, endurance; steadfastness; firm opinions, principles and unshakable goals are the "royal" traits.

Leonard Bernstein, *Conductor, Career Hexagram 15.*
The life of this world-famous American man of music is described in Personality Hexagram 15 as that of a traveller, a wanderer constantly setting new goals for himself — and reaching them.

For the conductor Bernstein all doors seem to open by themselves because among many other qualities he possesses sovereignty and humility.

Richard von Weizsäcker, *politician (Politiker),*
Career Hexagram 55.
Personality Hexagram 22 belongs to von Weizsäcker, marking him as an keen and critical observer with a highly developed standard of esthetics.

As a politician Career Hexagram 55 speaks of the high esteem he enjoys at the peak of his career.

Carl Gustav Jung, *psychologist (Psychologe), Career*
Hexagram 38.
Hexagram 61 depicts his personality, which is capable of complex and certain ascertainment of people and circumstances, and of acting from the heart. His ethical and spiritual greatness make him an unforgettable human being.

As a psychologist Jung developed an analytical eye for relationships, which in the sense of personality make-up made him ideal for his career.

And what if everyone were named 'John Smith'?

Naturally we must always appraise the contents of a Career Hexagram (as later on also those of the Compatibility Hexagrams) in the light of an individual's social and psychological environment. A name is not the determining factor for a profession, and it is highly improbable that all of the people named John Smith would be interested in pursuing identical careers, or that they'd all be qualified for it. For this reason I also refer to the personality profile based on name and date of birth in the interpretation examples shown, which can easily be checked. This obviously makes the analysis more precise and "personal".

2. The Situation

A. The System of Event Hexagrams

An Event Hexagram is constructed from the Name Trigram (= lower trigram) and the Date Trigram (= upper trigram) to which is added the birthday and date of the day in question (both calculated separately) in the sequence of day/month/year, reduced, as before, to one digit.

The hexagram rubrics "The Situation" and "Advice" should then be consulted.

Examples of Addition and Interpretation

Event Hexagram for NEIL ARMSTRONG, born August 5, 1930, for July 20, 1969, the day on which he became the first human being to set foot on the moon.

Dates
for the Date Trigram

5.	8.	1930
20.	7.	1969
25	15	3899	= ☰ (≡ symbol)
7	6	29
7	6	11
7	6	2

Date Trigram (above)

CHEN ☳ 34: The Great Might

Name Trigram (below)
Neil Armstrong

QIAN ☰

Neil Armstrong's Event Trigram 34 is identical with his Personality Hexagram. "The Great Might", the main qualities of his personality, not only manifest themselves continuously throughout his life, but were significant factors on that day when he landed on the moon. In hexagram 34 "The Situation" says: "You are the center of interest, and will be watched closely to see what you will be doing next." The entire world was watching.

Event Hexagram for KAROL WOJTYLA, better known as Pope John Paul II, born May 18, 1920, on May 13, 1981, the day an attempt was made on his life in St. Peter's Square in the Vatican City. (His Name Trigram is QIAN).

Dates
for the Date Trigram

18.	5.	1920
13.	5.	1981
31	10	3901	= ☳
4	1	13
4	1	4

Date Trigram (above)   KAN   ▦ 5: Considered

Name Trigram (below)   Waiting
Karol Wojtyla

Event Hexagram 5: Considered Waiting. The Date Trigram KAN already signals danger, and "The Situation" is described as one in which the Pope should remain calm and trust in help. He was, in fact, severely injured in the assassination attempt and immediate immobilisation and transport to a nearby hospital was required to prevent his condition turning grave. That he would survive the attempt on his life is indicated by the "Advice", according to which the waves would calm down again.

B. The System of the Influence Hexagram

In an Influence Hexagram the lower three lines are always represented by the Name Trigram, upon which the trigram is constructed reflecting the influence factor (an address, a vacation spot, food, a book title, a company name, etc.). Combined they become the Event Hexagram.

The system is the same as when constructing a Personality or Career Hexagram, and therefore need not be described again in detail.

Possible combinations:

Occasionally it may be advisable to link up certain Cognitograms with each other. For instance then, when we wish to prepare ourselves better for an upcoming situation or seek better understanding of a past occurrence.

In this case we consult all available sources of information, such as the Personality Hexagrams of all people involved, their Event and Influence Hexagrams for that particular day, the compatibility of the participants among themselves, etc.

Event Hexagram and Influence Hexagram of Historical Dates

The TITANIC, christened on May 31, 1911. In the course of her maiden voyage the British luxury liner struck an iceberg on April 14, 1912 and sank that night, carrying 1513 passengers to their death.

Event Hexagram 9: The Hindrance. "The Situation" and the "Advice" indicate that the Titanic should not have been under way on this date, therefore should not have started on the trip.

Influence Hexagram 34: The Great Might. The same two rubrics speak of a power struggle that ended fatally for the ship and its passengers.

Please check the hexagrams named in order to form your own opinion and discover additional interpretations.

Benjamin Franklin, born January 17, 1706, was one of the 39 delegates that on September 17, 1787 set their names beneath what is today the world's oldest national constitution, the Constitution of the United States of America.

Event Hexgram 25: The Unexpected. "The Situation" reveals that Franklin was confronted by facts beyond his influence. His comment was that the Constitution contained parts which he could not agree with at the time, but that he was not sure that he would never agree with them.

Influence Hexagram 42: Multiplication. As this is also Benjamin Franklin's Personality Hexagram, not only do the sections "The Situation" and "Advice" indicate the predominant influences, but "The Person" and "Partnership" provide a glimpse of the personal feelings the statesman harbored on that historic day.

It is interesting to note that on that day the Influence Hexagram for the United States of America was *53: Development.*

How did Norma Jean die?

Marilyn Monroe was originally named *Norma Jean Baker,* born on June 1, 1926, and she died on August 4, 1962, perhaps due to an overdose of sleeping pills or of alcohol poisoning. Or perhaps her death was the result of clever manipulation — or of a combination of some or all of the above. Very few people know for sure precisely what happened.

Let us take a look at exerpts from her Cognitogram:

On August 4, 1962, Norma Jean Baker had Event Hexagram 44: The Meeting.
The Situation: It is unavoidable but good for you to be informed about the motives of a person close to you that you were not aware of before.
Advice: Do not permit yourself to become involved in dubious transactions.

On August 4, 1962, Norma Jean Baker had Influence Hexagram 18: The Restoration.
The Situation: You are expecting information from the I Ching regarding a matter that is about to dissolve by itself.
Advice: It is of vital importance for you not to become impatient or fearful now. Help is already on its way.

On August 4, 1962, Marilyn Monroe had Event Hexagram 25: The Unexpected.
The Situation: You will be confronted with a situation after the fact, and for once you did not know everything ahead of time.
Advice: If you react to events spontaneously and without second thought, everything will turn out to your advantage.

On August 4, 1962, Marilyn Monroe had Influence Hexagram 27: Nourishment.
The Situation: Your taste will change considerably, to your own surprise.
Advice: Carefully examine your eating habits, and occasionally

consult a doctor or a dentist for a check-up.

Perhaps this case in point will inspire you to construct combination Hexagrams of your own.

Last but not least: The information you receive from a hexagram will not and cannot always reflect your own subjective views. After all, the new system of cognition also offers new avenues of letting aspects become visible, which heretofore had remained concealed.

3. Partnership

The System of Compatibility Hexagrams

A Compatibility Hexagram is constructed using the Name Trigrams of the two persons involved. Since the upper or lower placement of the trigrams leads to two hexagrams, we obviously receive two sets of information: firstly, how our own subconscious appraises the other person, and secondly, how the partner evaluates us.

An ancient wisdom teaches us that if we wish to find out how another person thinks about us, we should place him or her above us for a while. That's how it should be: the lower trigram represents the person asking, the upper trigram his or her partner.

Only the hexagram rubric "Partnership" need be consulted, although in some cases "The Person" or perhaps "Advice" may round off the picture.

Note: In this case a person's original name (in case he or she uses others) should be used, and that including all given names (the way a baptismal record contains them) as is usual in wedding ceremonies.

Examples of Addition and Interpretation

Compatibility Hexagram of JOHANN WOLFGANG VON GOETHE and CHARLOTTE VON STEIN.
In order to construct the hexagram properly, the following type of question is recommended:
"What does X (= upper trigram) think about Y (= lower trigram?"

Compatibility Hexagram of Famous Persons

Biographical Background

When Goethe met Charlotte von Stein in 1775, he was still seven years away from nobility and a new Name Trigram, and Compatibility Hexagram 29 ruled for them, more or less through mutual attitude. Considering the fact that *Frau* von Stein was married, this could well be interpreted for her as the fascination of the forbidden. But how differently did Charlotte, nee von Schardt, think about her future husband, Baron Friedrich von Stein! Hexagram 28 shows that she certainly expected fidelity and affection from him, which, seen from his point of view, was to bring on difficulties, as foretold by hexagram 61. And they did set in. The marriage was not a happy one. Charlotte von Stein, as she was now called, felt dissatisfied, as shown by hexagram 48, because according to hexagram 59 husband Friedrich devoted himself more to social and other obligations than to her. Now hexagram 7 shows that Johann Wolfgang von Goethe considered a partnership with Charlotte von Stein ideal, whereas she, according to hexagram 8, also had her mind set firmly on this union. Yet a marriage between the two would also not have been particularly happy. Hexagram 36 shows clearly that he could not imagine a Charlotte Goethe, and in hexagram 35 we see that she also nurtured no ambitions of this sort. In fact, a very dear and mellow friendship continued to connect the two after Goethe met Christiane Vulpius in 1788, who incidentally had the same Name Trigram as Charlotte Goethe would have. So it comes as no surprise that following their marriage Goethe considered the union to be less than ideal, as described by hexagram 11, and in hexagram 12 Christiane reveals what was missing in their partnership: mutual respect.

Part III

Hexagrams 1 through 64 Interpretation

Human Nature
is Basically Good

In all of the hexagrams I characterized "The Person" positively. This means, of course, that you could think differently from case to case. However, according to the Law of Resonance ("What we sow, that we shall reap") a person enters into a connection with precisely what he thinks, and accordingly with what he criticizes. And so we inadvertently obstruct in ourselves precisely those positive qualities that we are in doubt about in another person. One could go so far as to say that negative judgement turns us negative ourselves, and also draws corresponding situations and people into our lives.

So it is up to us to begin to create pleasant, positive experiences with people. That means we should all make an effort to maintain objectivity, and it tells us:

Superficial layers must be scraped away.

Gold is often panned in the mud.

Diamonds don't look like diamonds when they are found.

Treasures often have to be dug for.

The more candles I light in a dark room, the brighter it gets.

The positive degree of a person's reaction depends on the positive degree of your approach. Herein lies the Secret of Resonance.

Mo Ti, the founder of the Motistic school of philosophy in China in the 4th Century B.C., taught all-encompassing love among human beings and postulated: "Human nature is basically good." When seen this way, the world suddenly grows a lot brighter.

1
The Creative Power

The Person

You have tremendous energy at your disposal, based on a high potential for creativity. You have talent and the chance to achieve great things and benefits for mankind. Your place is at the top, and your way there as well as the fulfillment of your special task necessitate absolute purity of thought and action. Your creative achievements carry your spirit, and for that reason they must serve positive goals for the common good only.

The Situation

The time has come for your personal revolution. From now on, cast everything secondary aside and concentrate on essentials. Be aware that everything you do from now on will leave traces, and not only in your own life. They are tracks into which others will step in order to follow you. You must set an example in every way and sense.

Partnership

If your relationship is to be ideal and stay that way, you will have to reduce your claim to leadership. Give your partner the freedom to develop, and thus become a stronger companion for you. Recognize that by choosing this path you will not become weaker, but individually stronger instead.

Advice

Do not hesitate to transform your ideas and plans into action now. Otherwise you will pass up what is usually called the chance of a lifetime. If you are not sure about what details you should be taking care of, consult a person whom you respect for his integrity — or consult the I Ching.

2
The Receiving

The Person

You know what you want, and that is a lot. In order to reach your goal you are quite willing to employ several means: your passionate will, your personal charisma — and outside help. When you have overestimated your possibilities you spend a great deal of energy finding someone else to blame, which of course blocks your own way. The principle of give and take could, however, work wonders in your life.

The Situation

The time for half-finished things is past. In order to act without making mistakes you must now develop the high art of seeing beyond the obvious, of recognizing correlations, and of realizing when it is important not to act. You should seek advice and then accept it in order to be able to take possession of that which was always meant for you.

Partnership

The primary responsibility for maintaining your partnership lies with you. Which does not mean that things always have to develop along the lines you envisioned. Particularly now it is up to you to prove yourself worthy of a love, and to return it as an equal partner. Equal means that you have recognized the value of the other person and are convinced of it in your innermost soul.

Advice

Open yourself to others so that positive impulses can enter through the door of your heart. Think about your own position in your life, and that in the lives of others.

3
Difficulty starting

The Person

Your theater's wardrobe is often overloaded; that makes it easy for you to lose touch with reality. There is no role that you can play continuously all of your life — but you could just be yourself from now on. And only from that point on will it be possible to love you the way you are, and precisely that is what you really want.

The Situation

Being open toward others is the only thing that can help you now, because if someone is not aware of your problems, he or she will not be able to offer you solutions. If you accept the present situation and thereby yourself, your difficulties will soon be mastered and you will have stabilized yourself.

Partnership

Beginning a new is always difficult, but can also be very rewarding. Do not demand more of your partner than you are able to give yourself. Perhaps you won't be able to implement this right away, but fortunately you can learn it.

Advice

Set new priorities and your thicket of problems will disentangle itself. What you need most now is clear vision.

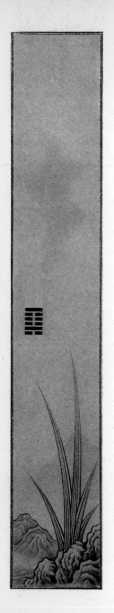

4
Inexperience

The Person

Between dream and reality one can meet a truly lovely person: you. Life is a big game for you in which it is perfectly alright to make a mistake anytime, or even lose once in a while. When you meet someone who doesn't 'play' you become confused and sad and flee into the role of the hurt victim. But in spite of all of this you know that you are playing, and that you are learning — for that day on which the game turns serious.

The Situation

Nobody blames you for your inexperience — except perhaps you yourself. Go ahead and trust in an older person with enough experience to find you a workable way in the present situation. Because only when you realize that you know nothing will you be able to act effectively.

Partnership

Your personal relations are consigned to fate in joyful innocence — and they stay joyful. If you and your partner would allow each other time, a relationship of yours might very possibly have a future.

Advice

Many aspects of your being would like to be recognized by you as well as by the people close to you. Be open for new experiences that could enrich your life and help you to cope with unusual situations.

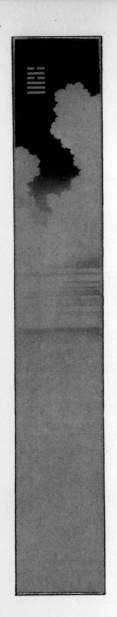

5
Considered Waiting

The Person

The train in which you are riding is moving too fast for you to observe the landscape through which you are travelling; it is the train of your life. In other words, the greater your haste to make certain life experiences, the less you are aware of the path that you are taking.

The Situation

Retain your serenity no matter what threatens to happen. The only real danger for you lies in losing your nerves. If, however, you manage to signal confidence, you will become untouchable, will gain surety and very quickly receive aid from an unexpected source.

Partnership

Your partner and you must now stick closer together than ever before, because your relationship is being attacked by forces that are beyond your influence at this time. Use the foreknowledge that the attacks will be extremely unfair to build a protective wall that will protect you both.

Advice

Since you have no direct control over the forces working on you, avoid heading for a confrontation. On the contrary: do nothing, wait. The waves will calm down.

6
The Conflict

The Person

You manage to win friends one moment, and make enemies the next. Although you have enough self-confidence to let an opinion other than your own stand, do not react to every provocation with your own inimitable equanimity. The result could be differences that may lead to bridges being torn down.

The Situation

In your personal sphere you are being confronted by a disappointment, and it looks as if a break in relations could occur. Your rights or certain demands can under no circumstances be manifested at this time.

Partnership

Agree with your partner that each of you belongs to himself, and not to the other person. Rules and regulations will merely destroy the necessary basis of voluntary togetherness that a happy partnership needs.

Advice

Be moderate in your words and actions. Ask a neutral person for advice before you say or do things that are final.

7
Gathered Strength

The Person

Your responsibilities in life and to yourself are clear to you. When you follow ideals you do so with your unerring sense of what is real. But you also know that you will be subjected to attacks that increase in proportion to your own ethical development. Your personal test consists of simply letting things happen without rebelling against them.

The Situation

Your goals are of interest to others, too. Share them and bring them into accordance with the intentions of the society or group in question. To your own surprise you will then discover a new way that you can travel joyfully — and certainly not alone.

Partnership

You are beyond any doubt an ideal couple. Your partnership would, however, be even more ideal if you granted each other a bit more freedom of movement.

Advice

Be generous toward the people around you. This attitude will provide you with all of the strength you need, and protect you more effectively against verbal or mental attacks.

8
Union

The Person

Some consider you extrovert, others introvert. The truth is that you are both, and will not consider this contradictory as long as there is such a thing as high tide and low tide. Of course it would be helpful for your social relations if you would initiate others into your personal philosophy in order to make yourself more "calculable".

The Situation

You are faced with a far-reaching decision involving your accepting a great deal of responsibility. If you have the least bit of doubt about your ability to do justice to the mission in question, you must refuse it! For your own assurance, consult the I Ching in this matter.

Partnership

In a sense, you are what holds this partnership together and who is responsible for it. Remember each day anew the all-conquering power of "we".

Advice

Especially in times in which you set out to conquer new worlds you need strong social ties to something that will support you psychically. But when you have it, nothing can or will stand in your way.

9
The Hindrance

The Person

Your motto says all or nothing at all. When you commit yourself, you often overdo it and plunge into overwork. Whether or not your efforts are acknowledged is of no importance to you. You are motivated by the desire to be of help.

The Situation

There is no way foreward and no way back. Wherever you turn, hindrances block your moves. And this is good the way it is, because success is definitely waiting for you, yet if you were to reach it too soon, you would not appreciate your good fortune and therefore not know how to hold on to it.

Partnership

It would never occur to you to turn down a request voiced by your partner. But if you are opposed to it in your innermost being, you should critically examine your motives for maintaining the partnership, because without sincerity on your part it will not last long.

Advice

Do not undertake new endeavors at this time, no matter how tempting a chance may appear. The time for it is not right yet. Wait calmly and keep your thoughts to yourself. Conducting yourself in this manner will bring you prestige along with the awaited success.

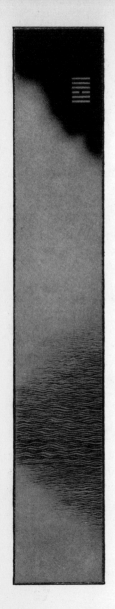

10
Behavior

The Person

Your desire for harmony is clear to others that influence you positively, and can help guard you against false moves. You understand the people around you and often know their plans and intentions ahead of time. This enables you to act self-confidently and makes you a valued advisor, friend and partner.

The Situation

A thunderstorm usually does not take place with the intention of killing anyone, but people's conduct lastly decides whether or not this happens. The present situation is similar: if you retain your poise and remain calm und unobtrusive, no harm will come to you. If, however, you decide to expose yourself and attract attention, this could bring about your destruction.

Partnership

You are no longer taking each other particularly seriously, and therefore not giving each other the necessary minimum of respect. Since this does not cause you suffering, there is the danger that you may soon feel superior, and irresponsibly let the relationship end.

Advice

For a short period of time, the length of which you will be able to determine intuitively, reduce your demands and expectations to a bare minimum. In order to influence your environment you will have to learn to adjust to it.

11
Prospering

The Person

Your sensitivity feels the nearing of favorable constellations, and therefore you do not hesitate to make use of your chance. And since you will be in harmony with cosmic law in what you are undertaking, you will find loyal friends and helpers that will help bring your plans to fruition.

The Situation

Professional success is close at hand. You have a great deal of healing influence on others and are close to realizing your most audacious plans. Everything that happens from now on, every person that you meet, appears to be a welcome piece of the puzzle of your intentions.

Partnership

There is a lot that you unnecessarily withhold from your partner. More trusting confidence would prevent many a misunderstanding.

Advice

It is of decisive importance for your future that you learn to accept and heed that even the tallest mountain would stand senselessly alone without the deepest valley beside it. Never become careless on the narrow paths that lead you higher. And when you have reached the top, remember your old friends.

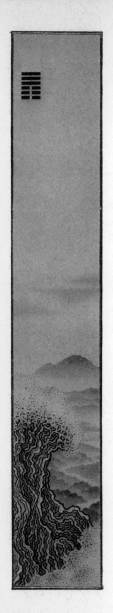

12
The Standstill

The Person

You require a great deal of love, but you will not admit it. Instead you prefer to arrange things so that the whole world has to care for you and show you respect in one way or another. And if this tactic sometimes fails, you withdraw with hurt feelings. Your self-confidence is really very susceptible. And this although you have in you all of the qualities needed to love and be loved in return.

The Situation

When you are part of a traffic jam you can observe how everyone is in everyone else's way without actually wanting to be. The situation you are in is similar to this. Nobody wants to hinder you personally. You are in the middle of a collective experience that has to do with relationships on a higher plane connected with the cosmic order. And you will recognize that the calmness that each participant manages to muster finally determines the progress made by all.

Partnership

You are now reacting toward each other with irritation. Soon you will realize that you have treated your partner unjustly. In the future you will show each other greater respect.

Advice

Because you judge people and situations too quickly, you often miss the purpose behind a given event. Devote yourself to the study of analogies and you will become an objective observer who is always aware of the right course of action.

13
Togetherness

The Person

Although you enjoy living the role of a recluse, you know how to work together with the right people at the right time. You also possess the rare talent of being able to employ your integrity as your only capital against the dangers usually inherent in new ventures.

The Situation

You are facing a decisive step in the development of your personality. You must act now, or else fate will act for you. If your intentions serve the needs of society you will achieve great things shortly, but not by yourself! Make sure that you have the extensive support of older and experienced people.

Partnership

Agreement between you and your partner is exceptionally great, which lends your relationship firmness and strength in every situation. When outside influences beset you, the two of you are truly one single entity.

Advice

If you are unsure in your choice of helpers in view of the special character of the present situation, decide the way a revered ancestor of yours would have.

14
Prosperity

The Person

Energy, competence, authority. All three interlock, and together they form the engine that moves you. You are constantly in action and extraordinarily successful. Your greatest asset, however, and at the same time the main reason for your success, is your humble, natural personality, your ability to see the good in every person and not to judge superficially.

The Situation

You hold the last pieces of the puzzle of greatest happiness in your hand. Shortly you will attain prosperity and prestige. Yet fortune will test you: you will be given in order to give unto others. If you let others share your abundance and remain the person you are, fortune will be yours faithfully, and you will even be able to multiply your wealth.

Partnership

Being blessed by fortune in all other areas, you are convinced that in your partnership, too, things could not be better. But instead of flowers, love and time you give your partner successes. You have not been aware of this, but now that you know, you will have to do something about it.

Advice

Think of all of the people that have contributed to your being what you are today. Be generous toward them, and stay humble in spite of your tremendous success. Do not overdo anything.

15
Moderation

The Person

You have the ability to hold on to whatever you once possess. The reason for this is your humility. You do not flaunt your possessions, and when you enjoy a feeling of pride, you do so quietly in your mind. When you want to reach something, your calm, reserved personality and the fascinating surety you exude open all doors for you.

The Situation

At the time it is important for you to be tolerant and to act diplomatically. The situation demands that all participants hold back their claims, which is not as easy a matter for others as it is for you. If you manage to set an example now you will have qualified yourself for a leading position that one would like to discuss with you, as soon as things have resumed their normal course again.

Partnership

It may be true that you can evaluate a set of circumstances better at this time than your partner can, but the most important thing is that he or she has the feeling of having reached a decision without your assistance. Remain tactfully in the background.

Advice

Do not permit yourself to over-react by way of disputes or law suits. You would lose, even if you were right.

16
Enthusiasm

The Person

Moving ahead analytically would really spoil your fun, and you do not want to risk that. Therefore you act according to your feelings and accept the fact that a flash in the pan is of short duration. Yet you certainly do take life seriously, contrary to the opinion a lot of people have of you. Your optimism never falters, and it helps you to solve many a problem.

The Situation

Soon you will undertake something new and pursue it in a disciplined manner unusual for you. In this particular phase you could even be lucky at games of chance or financial speculations. Listen to your inner voice, which is presently talking to you louder than usual.

Partnership

You know how to cast a spell over people. Consider carefully if you want to play, and if so, if you can answer for it to others than yourself.

Advice

However things turn out for you in the next few weeks, handle your money conscientiously and spend sparingly. Be cautious in your choice of friends.

17
The Succession

The Person

You take people and things the way they are, knowing full well what is going on behind the scenes. Precisely that is your reason for being discreet and very willing to adjust. This makes you a valued friend and adviser.

The Situation

Someone is about to stand in your way and you will easily find out who it is: swim with the current. Whoever is not following you is coming at you.

Partnership

Although your love for each other is of primary importance to you and your partner, you will have to discuss a number of differences in your respective value systems in order to avoid later conflicts.

Advice

Serve a cause that is meant to serve you at a later time, and only then will it be of use to you.

18
The Restoration

THE PERSON

When it comes to dealing with problems, you know just about all of the tricks and dodges. But unintentionally you have tricked yourself: as long as you cleverly manage to avoid the trials of life, they will always reappear before you clothed in different circumstances — until you have mastered them once and for all. And in this lies a very special "magic" that can make you free.

THE SITUATION

You are expecting information from the I Ching regarding a matter that is about to dissolve by itself. Do not undertake anything to halt this development, because only when you find the strength to "let go" deep inside of you, can that enter into your life that is destined for you, and for which the time is now ripe.

PARTNERSHIP

Accept the hand that is being offered you. You have been forgiven and someone wants to help you forgive yourself.

ADVICE

It is of vital importance for you not to become impatient or fearful now. Help is already on its way.

19
The Nearing

The Person

You are farsightedly and cleverly arranging things, so that you will be in control no matter which turn events take. You do have well-founded knowledge, although it revolves around a given purpose. That is how you make yourself indispensable, even as a friend. However, less perfectionism would help you to recognize who your real friends are.

The Situation

What you have long hoped for is finally happening: your capabilities are being recognized and respected. You are being supported and promoted. But be on your guard: as early as autumn (some translations of the I Ching indicate August) there will be an attempt to contest your new position.

Partnership

You want to dominate in your partnership, which is agreeable to your partner. One day, however, you will find it boring to always receive a "yes" as an answer, never a "no". There is still time to correct the situation and to establish a basis that will insure that the two of you have something to say to each other in the future.

Advice

Avoid creating envy or making enemies. Stay within reasonable limits when you acquire things, travel or pursue your hobbies. Grant people that ask you for it your help.

20
Observation

The Person

If one were to consult a psychosomatic key that decodes psychic causes of physical ailments, it would very probably reveal that you are suffering from faulty vision. Either you are playing at observing, and only see what you want to see, or you are playing looking away, and are still seeing more than you actually wanted to. Both cases lead to your not seeing yourself and life realistically, your not yet having accepted the "Challenge of Life". You would be well advised to entrust yourself to someone who can take your fear of life away and instill you with self-confidence. Without knowing it, you have also closed your eyes to the beautiful sides of life and require something like courage in order to not see a sun flower as a monster.

The Situation

A change is taking shape. You may be changing addresses soon, or else you may be given the chance to advance professionally.

Partnership

Your relationship with your partner is harmonious and well-balanced in every way. Your partner is the only human being whom you trust without any reservation whatsoever.

Advice

Since other people are now approaching you especially well-disposed because of interesting ideas that you have brought forth, you should not consider an offer too sceptically. People are on your side and want to help you to get a good start. Of course everyone involved will benefit from the matter, but you deserve the lion's share.

21
Prevailing Against Odds

The Person

Unusual situations require unusual measures. In this case fate has definitely found the right person in you: you are a natural strategist that knows how to act and re-act. You find a way out of precarious situations with the sureness of a sleepwalker, and one could only wish to have someone like you at one's side.

The Situation

You must find out as quickly as possible who or what is hindering you at the time. When you do, you will experience the help of a friend who won't make an issue of it if you make a mistake. He will help you in a way that will prevent your making the same mistake again.

Partnership

You should end a relationship in which someone is consciously treating you incorrectly. If, however, the relationship in question is your personal one, the two of you will have to work out a mutual way.

Advice

Put yourself in touch with positive vibrations by thinking and acting positively. That sounds simpler than it is — but the effect is also stronger than you might imagine. Circumstances will develop in your favor. Stay peaceable and confident.

22
Loveliness

The Person

You are an excellent, critical observer and can discern structures, facets, colors, nuances, the entirety and every single detail. Under certain circumstances this capability causes you pain, as you are an absolute esthete and register your environment with extreme sensitivity. You solve problems elegantly and consistently on a high level.

The Situation

What matters here is the form and not the content. This coincides excellently with your intentions. You manage to enhance your position, although not your authority. For changes beyond this, the time has not come yet.

Partnership

The expectations you have in each other are founded primarily on esthetics and sophisticated flirtation. A lot more could become of it, if you would begin acting naturally.

Advice

The harmony that you perceive is deceptive. Everyone is now his own best friend. Make an effort to help others and put your personal expectations aside for awhile. Nothing could hold you back more at this time than a catalogue of wants.

23
Deterioration

The Person

You are continually getting into extreme situations because of your carefree way of going about life. But you invariably rise again and start anew at the beginning. It would easily be possible for you to influence your fate at any given point, but you need danger — and the miracle that then has to happen promptly.

The Situation

You are the captain of a sinking ship, and you know it. All you can do now and in any case must do, is to consciously not worry about yourself and instead concentrate on the welfare of others with increased vigor. To paraphrase the situation: only by letting the crew and passengers disembark can you lighten your ship enough to keep it afloat until help arrives. A break is about to occur in your life, but it will be very healthy for you. The new situation already waiting for you beyond the present one will bring you additional joy and success.

Partnership

If you are incapable of entering into a compromise that would do justice to both of you, you should end the relationship.

Advice

Retain your serenity, whatever happens. Do not listen to people trying to spread panic. Someone is interested in seeing that you now commit an error.

24
The New Beginning

The Person

You have learned from your own mistakes and those of others, but this is strictly your own concern, so you return to your defensive position in hedgehog-manner. Besides, you want peace and quiet and consider it totally superfluous that someone should have a closer look into your life and personal sphere. Hardly anyone knows you well enough to objectively behave properly in respect to you. It is enough for you that the person you love manages this.

The Situation

A new dawn in your life. The night is past. Now the time for the New is at hand, a new cycle is beginning its orbit. It could be that you are convalescing following a long illness, are about to find a new job, change professions or will meet the partner of your life. Whatever the new factor in your life will be: you will now realize that there is a wise principle of order that acts behind everything, and that nothing happens purely by coincidence.

Partnership

You are either getting to know the right partner for you, or an established partnership is about to gain new perspectives.

Advice

Do not rush anything merely because the events are so fascinating and new. Every seed needs time to germinate.

25
The Unexpected

The Person

You enjoy perfecting ideas, making things transparent, and manage to unlock secrets for yourself. You apply the knowledge that you gain in very original ways that often astound the people around you. Take care, though, not to hurt anyone's feelings.

The Situation

You will be confronted with a situation after the fact, and for once you did not know everything ahead of time. Your assumptions were headed into a completely wrong direction — luckily for you, however.

Partnership

At present your partner is having a difficult time identifying your wishes and plans, which complicates your relationship. It is up to you to become more equable, more calculable.

Advice

If you react to events spontaneously and without second thought, everything will turn out to your advantage.

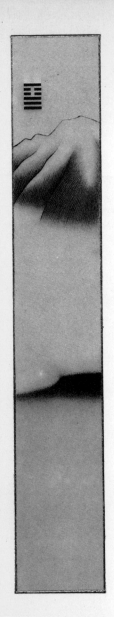

26
The Great Taming Power

The Person

You observe and analyse calmly, keep secrets to yourself and walk a straight path. But precisely this is what makes the people around you nervous and lets them react suspiciously towards you. Yet anyone who has comprehended you will never again have to fear being without a friend when he or she is in trouble. You are a rock in the surging tide.

The Situation

You have the knowledge and the means of realizing a project that will be beneficial to the community. However, things are not moving ahead at the time because third parties are trying to see their personal interests realized. You will recognize these people and their intentions, however, and react sovereignly.

Partnership

Your partner is in perfect agreement with you. It is therefore of great importance that you justify this high degree of love and trust. Observe yourself critically from time to time.

Advice

You hold all of the reins in your hands when you appear calm and serene. People expect you to explode and are in no way prepared for a totally opposite reaction.

27
Nourishment

The Person

"You are what you eat" is a popular saying, and it has an important parallel on a mental level. Whatever you readily accept as input in the way of ideas, concepts, events and their combined effects, also influences your behavior and thusly your life and life-experience. Often you are dissatisfied without knowing why. You are literally famished for harmony, for positive experience — and yet it would be so easy for you to have all of this.

The Situation

Your taste will change considerably, to your own surprise, and that will usher in a new chapter of your life. Your concept of values will then be different from what it once was. You will grow humbler and happier.

Partnership

Your partnership should be intact and firm enough for the two of you to now talk openly about wishes not articulated so far.

Advice

Carefully examine your eating habits, and occasionally consult a doctor or a dentist for a check-up. At the same time it is advisable to curb or break off contact to people who have little in the way of positive things to tell you.

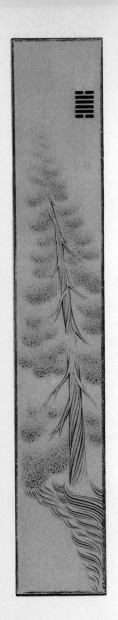

28
Excess

The Person

Your heart jumps for joy at the thought that the world has you!
This generosity of thought, alas, is not fully appreciated by
everyone. Indeed, it may be obstructing precisely those ways,
that you really wanted to travel. If you would become less inac-
cessible, you could achieve a great deal more in life.

The Situation

You have filled the measure to the rim and should not be surprised that it is now overflowing. But someone will be there to help
you find a larger vessel for the future — if you will admit that you
overestimated yourself in the matter.

Partnership

Faithfulness on your part would simplify things a lot, and make
a number of your questions superfluous.

Advice

Stay courteous and to the point and do not attempt to make
others responsible for something that was entirely your matter.

29
Danger

The Person

You sense dangers, but you do not fear them. This gives you the advantage and makes you unassailable. You win, therefore, because you make conflict superfluous. And only then.

The Situation

Your immediate surroundings bear danger for you that is connected with a loss. Through your tried and proven lack of fear, however, you can render your opponent powerless and in countering actually use him to aid you in realizing your goals.

Partnership

At the time you are provoking a crisis just to reassure yourself of your partner's love. That is not fair, and the other person could learn from your conduct…

Advice

The more you remain above any reproach, the stronger will be the protection you enjoy. Irreproachability, by the way, also means that it is not up to you to condemn others.

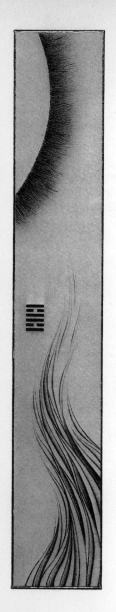

30
The Fire

The Person

You are a distinct personality and know it. That may open doors for you, but it can also close hearts. In cases like this you actually manage to burn bridges behind you with a tear in your eye. Having to deal with you won't be pleasantly exciting until you feel loved or have arrived socially.

The Situation

Someone is dishonest with you and is trying to present you a matter distortedly. This saddens you, but at the same time finally puts you in the position of being able to take rigorous action. From this liberating objectivity you draw strength.

Partnership

Various rumors about your partnership are making the rounds, but this does not faze you in the least, and soon the rumors will cease to be heard.

Advice

It would be wise at this time to seek the advice of a friend or other person loyal to you.

31
The Attraction

The Person

Your type of person is a rarity in a way. You are objective, logical, reasonable, correct, and therefore calculable for your environment. Your uprightness earns you respect and high esteem.

The Situation

The hour is at hand. You will draw sucess unto yourself in a measure that you had not dared hope for. Your strong emotional attachment to the person or matter in question now acts like a magnet that draws things to it once they are close enough.

Partnership

Love makes people blind, and that for a simple reason: the closer they come, the less they see of each other. At the time, however, you probably don't think much of the idea of keeping a bit more distance in order to gain a better view and appraisal of each other. Too bad, because if you did you would discover things that would please you very much.

Advice

You are the one that has to take the first step. The clearer it becomes that you are now in action, the more will people make an effort to oblige you.

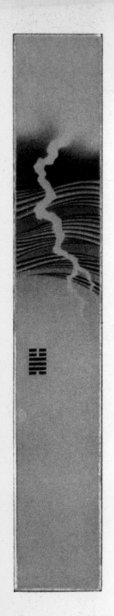

32
The Duration

The Person

Loyalty, perseverance, steadfastness, firm opinions and principles, and unshakable goals. This is you. And this makes you successful — on a long-term basis.

The Situation

You have been in a situation like the present one before. And now you can again act the way you did then. But you will have to ascertain which of the two ways availing themselves is still solid beneath the surface.

Partnership

You augment each other fabulously, are really "made for one another". Your partnership is founded on high and lasting values.

Advice

There is nothing wrong with your sticking to things that you are familiar with and that have proven themselves. But perhaps there is a possibility of doing it with an additional touch of spice and spirit. The duration, left to itself, would bore itself; it needs new impulses.

33
The Withdrawal

The Person

Pressure generates counter-pressure, and that you know how to avoid. You maintain peace in your internal and external affairs and recognize the moment when you can withdraw without haste or loss of face. In this manner you are always at the right place at the right time — at least in safety.

The Situation

Your opponents are strong and unfair. Avoid any sort of confrontation; withdraw instead. The opinions these people have need not concern you. Following your withdrawal you will meet with unusual people and circumstances through which you will be successful.

Partnership

For once do without having to have your way. That will make two people a lot happier — one of them being you.

Advice

Nobody can climb up a smooth wall. Do not reveal your feelings, maintain stoical calm on the outside.

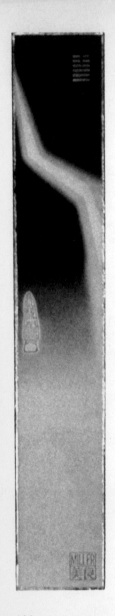

The Person

You live with a high degree of responsibility, because you are powerful. Your influence on people and situations is enhanced by your personal charisma. This is your life-long test of character. If you successfully recognize and accept the weaknesses which you certainly have, you will be able to accept them in others, and never misuse your power.

The Situation

You are the center of interest, and will be watched closely to see what you will be doing next. If you remain "one of the inner circle", you will have won. He who would rule must first be capable of serving, an old Chinese proverb tells us.

Partnership

Whoever influences someone also carries the responsibility for that person's development. A bit more initiative on his or her part would be good for your partner, and lastly for you, too.

Advice

Your influence will not wane if you do not exercise it all of the time. Be careful that in a trial of strength you are not the one who has to prove himself.

35
Progress

The Person

As long as you believe in yourself, nothing can stand in your way. This realization is your greatest stock, and with it you will be able to convince others of your ideas and capabilities. If you retain your humility in spite of this, you will one day bring forth great achievements.

The Situation

Your ascent is beginning. But be careful: later you will be judged by the way you reached the top. Use the opportunity to help others without securing a service in return or expecting one. Divide and rule, the motto reads.

Partnership

Each of you should have a bit more leisure for yourselves. If you would grant each other more personal freedom, the problems between you would cease to be.

Advice

It is not enough to have a clear vision of the goal; one also has to know the way to it. In your case it is brotherly love and fairness.

36
Eclipse of Light

The Person

Everything dark and mysterious has a strong fascination for you. You study the darkness because one does not have to fear what one knows. One could think you were practicing "whistling in the dark". Very few people are aware that what drives you on is the search for the meaning of life, the search for light.

The Situation

Remain in the background. Things are not happening according to your wishes at the time, and if you get involved, you could only make them worse. Prepare a plan for yourself, but do not discuss it with anybody.

Partnership

Your ideals do not match. This is the main reason for all of your misunderstandings and differences. You can only solve the problem by granting your partner a greater right to a personal opinion and by beginning to show him or her some respect.

Advice

You are what you think. Your complexes are absolutely unnecessary. If you were to see yourself positively, others would automatically conduct themselves open and friendly towards you.

37
The Family

The Person

You do whatever you want to — if and when you happen to know what you want. Fear of failure serves you as a frequent alibi for not undertaking anything in the first place. That describes the situation if you are living alone.

In the community of others you come to life. When you sense security and order, you feel confident and courageous and immediately strong enough to take charge. You require a great deal of attention and care in order to recognize your mission in life and to fulfill it.

The Situation

Listen to your heart, it is telling you the truth. Someone is going to stand by you, but you will have to act by yourself. And your action will have to be in accordance with the situation in which you are. Take an intact, happy family as an example. Then you will know your place and mission.

Partnership

You can make progress if you try to solve the problem together. Get everything off your chest and be co-operative with your partner.

Advice

You are not alone and should not let your courage falter. Take the hand of the person who wants to pull you out of the mire, and can do it. This is no time for false pride!

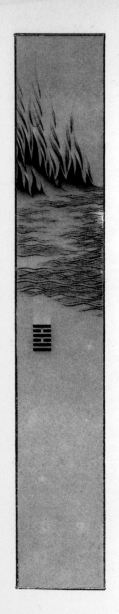

38
The Opposite

The Person

Whoever asks you for a clear decision receives two. The reason is that you have "x-ray vision" when it comes to the relativity of things, and you practise mental Jiu Jitsu between 'on the one hand' and 'on the other hand'. On the one hand you always seek to maintain balances, on the other hand you prevent your own personal mental balance by this particular way of going about things. You could be happier, if you accepted the fact that plus and minus cancel each other out when they appear simultaneously. Everything has its own time, its reason for being and its own purpose.

The Situation

Differences of opinion can be a peaceful manifestation of human thinking. But apparently people are not too interested in differences, although these are the result of their uniqueness, and that is why the varying opinions different people have paradoxically lead to conflicts. This is precisely the situation in which you find yourself at the moment, and you recognize how absurd certain people can act. This should put you at an advantage — and perhaps stimulate your humor.

Partnership

Your shyness is being interpreted incorrectly. Contrary to your usual habits, go ahead and take the initiative regarding your partner. You will see that making an effort will open up new avenues for you without any "ifs", "ands" or "buts".

Advice

Work at maintaining your neutrality and under no circumstances let yourself get involved in debates. Although you possess better insight into the correlations involved it will be better for you if for once others do not know your opinion.

39
The Blockade

The Person

A meaningful life to you means having a soul covered with creases and wrinkles. That is why time and again you draw special trials into your life and just as often approach them with the joyful determination and moral integrity to prevail. Having a person like you for a friend means finding adventure and protection at the same time.

The Situation

In a current matter you will meet with opposition. If you will remember a similar situation in the past, you will see the reason for this and also understand that you will sporadically be confronted by the basic problem, until you have mastered it in a perfect manner and have grown and developed in doing so.

Partnership

A third party has deliberately brought tension into your partnership; the motives should be apparent to you. Now it is important not to unintentionally permit this person to gain power over you, and that makes it absolutely necessary for you and your partner to remain calm and serene. Only then will you be truly unassailable.

Advice

When the flow of water is halted by an obstruction, the water does not retreat resignedly, nor does it react violently. It waits and remains calm. It gathers itself at the point of blockade, consolidates its power, and at last overflows the obstruction and continues on its way. Learn from this example.

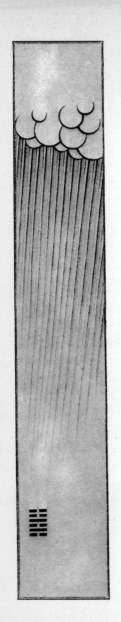

40
The Liberation

THE PERSON

Your dynamic manner sweeps one away — into chasms of sadness or up to the peaks of joy, depending on the moment. In any case, you are thorough. And highly esteemed, as a philosophical or explosively innovative adviser.

THE SITUATION

The phase of agitation, fear and obstruction is past. You can begin anew: enter into friendships, sign contracts, travel, find a new home, or start a new life if you wish. But whatever you plan to do: do it without hesitation. Only rarely in the course of time is fortune so generously inclined.

PARTNERSHIP

You will free yourself from the present situation. If your are in conflict with your partner, your differences will be reconciled; if the relationship hampers you, you will find a way of separating fairly.

ADVICE

Be especially watchful in all of your present actions that they originate from positive energy and harm no one. You may now recognize who your true friends are. Accept this realization gratefully, and forgive those who were incapable of friendship towards you.

41
Reduction

The Person

Unconcernedly you let yourself drift with the current of your moods, and you enjoy the fact that people just cannot be angry with you. You are very intensive in everything you do, which precludes that you will ever accept mediocrity.

The Situation

Your advantages are going up in smoke, material losses are now probable. Accept all of this; later, as the situation changes, you will recognize your progress.

Partnership

Suddenly you are no longer the hub of the universe for your partner. Your relationship stabilizes itself on a companionable level. Do not react to this with hurt, because soon the perspectives will change for you, too.

Advice

Whatever you have to face at this time, accept it and do not attempt to make the world around you believe that everything is the way it used to be. This would shut your door to reality and thereby obstruct your way into a new start.

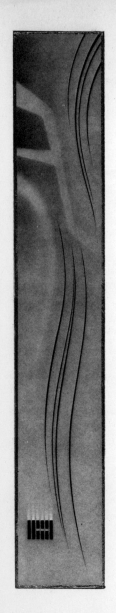

The Person

You comprehend quickly and are capable of seeing and appraising things in their greater context. This predestinates you for tasks that require firm decisions — such as leadership positions. But privately, too, many people consider your advice indispensable.

The Situation

The seed is about to germinate: what you had long hoped and planned for can now be realized. Unexected opportunities also present themselves, and not only can you, you must show now what you are capable of. "If not now, when?" is the motto.

Partnership

Because you have overestimated yourself, the expectations placed in your partner were also exaggerated. Show understanding and think about your continuing mutual way. Open yourself to let new impulses enter.

Advice

Take the advice of someone whose support you really had not counted on. Finally you will come to the conclusion that many people participated in bringing your good fortune about, and they should now have their share of it.

43
The Breakthrough

The Person

You posess a dormant talent that can be considered classic. One day — and no one will know better than you when that time has come — you will discard all social bonds and perhaps even standards, if necessary, in order to unfold in complete independence, to the joy and benefit of others, with whom from that moment on you will be in a steady exchange of positive power.

The Situation

Someone is employing and wasting a great deal of strength in order to prevent your breaking through. But the less you take notice of this, the less interesting you will be as an opponent for the person in question.

Partnership

You are finally able to recognize what brought conflicts about and who the adversary is. Now all of the problems can be solved gently and permanently.

Advice

Do not open doors by force. After all, you do have the masterkey.

44
The Meeting

The Person

Your subtle and unusually well founded knowledge of human nature plus your not always unintentionally employed charm bring you together with people that positively influence your life. You will be able to establish an extraordinarily successful enterprise and/or lead an extremely happy personal life.

The Situation

It is unavoidable but healthy for you to be informed about the motives of a person close to you that you were not aware of before. This enables you to intervene helpfully and, in a certain matter, to finally lay your cards on the table.

Partnership

"Not all are free who deride their chains", Lessing wrote. But you maneuvered yourself into the position you are now in. If you yield to a temper now, you are the person you once used to be — and soon alone again.

Advice

Do not permit yourself to become involved in dubious transactions. The person whom you would trust in this case, would himself already have been deceived.

45
The Collection

The Person

You place your trust in quantity. Your success lies in teamwork, your security in the gathering of material and spiritual values, your pleasure in companionable get-togethers. But the combinations listed here are interchangeable and therefore optimally appliable by you.

The Situation

You are meeting people who could render you valuable services, if you open yourself to their ideas and proposals, and are ready to co-operate with them in spite of initial obstructions.

Partnership

The intensity of your partnership is dependent on an association that one of you belongs to, and in which he or she invests disproportionate amounts of time. The time has come for a clean break.

Advice

Loyalty is expected of you — no more and no less. Do not affront anyone just because you feel overstrained at the moment.

46
The Ascent

The Person

You are successful because you think in terms of success. And because you help others, you also experience support through others. Your understanding of giving and receiving is well-balanced.

The Situation

Your modesty may be a precious jewel in the flashy contests of vanities, but the time has come for you to insist on your legal rights, and to claim the financial benefits that are due you. Do not hesitate any longer!

Partnership

Your motives are harmoniously united with those of your partner, and therefore the only thing still standing in the way of your mutual happiness is non-recognition.

Advice

You possess a great potential for letting others share in your success. Watch out, however, that your kindness is not exploited.

47
Distress

The Person

You enjoy sitting securely in your nutshell — and dream of people offering you their fondness or even love. But only if you discard the shell yourself can you prevent that particularly those people have to hurt you, that have been seeking closeness to you with the best of intentions.

The Situation

You feel yourself maneuvered into a situation from which you can only escape by fleeing into attack, causing deliberate confrontation. Through this, however, new perspectives will open up for you and direct your somewhat passive previous life into vigorous new channels that will strengthen you in every way.

Partnership

Loosen up your soul and finally be the person that your partner found in you even before you found yourself. Your way to the other person now leads through yourself.

Advice

Do not fight with words, but rather with silence. Your determination will speak for itself when the time is right for you to act.

48
The Well

The Person

Your nature can be compared to a spring that joyfully gives to all and neither asks how many jugs it fills nor worries about the water perhaps not being plentiful enough for all. This attitude is founded on spiritual depth, and harbors the knowledge of fulfilling a function for one's neighbor and the community.

The Situation

Once again someone is dependent on your help, but this time you are alone, others do not understand your commitment. Do not lose time trying to explain it. The circumstances require spontaneity and a certain discretion of the heart.

Partnership

You wish to delve deeply into you partner's secret, and do not know yet that in doing so you are only hoping to find yourself. Choosing this way is not unwise, but the timing is: right now your partner would prefer to learn to understand him or herself better.

Advice

Unexpected solutions will avail themselves if you look for analogies to the special situation in which you happen to be. The greater your understanding of the necessity of the process taking place, the easier it will be for you to find "comrades in spirit" to support your efforts.

49
The Upheaval

The Person

According to you, changes should not be anticipated but implemented instead. And that, if at all possible, at a time when no one expects them, best together with people possessing hearts and minds, and a goodly portion of both, if you please.

The Situation

One expects you to have considered not only the present but also the future. Now you can demonstrate one of your specialties: proceeding carefully, almost slowly — and yet acting with all of the energy available. The results will eventually bring you together with unusual people, which will lead to a radical change in your life.

Partnership

The so-called roles are no longer clearly defined, may have already been exchanged. And yet you will enjoy and learn to love the new character of your relationship.

Advice

You will have ample opportunity to realize your just claims. You should, however, avoid a private revolution. You will need your strength for other things.

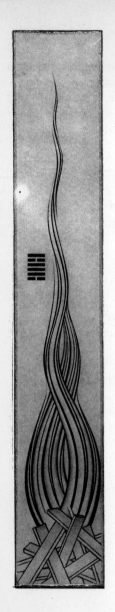

50
The Cosmic Order

The Person

With only a single one of your strong, positive thoughts you manage to light up a dark room. Your ethical and spiritual influence on people is lasting, if not to say forming. Since you act within the highest spiritual law, the Cosmic Order, you are not only aware of the responsibility this entails, but are very familiar with it.

The Situation

Although you hold the reins, you should work together with two helpers, because jointly you will have a karmic mission of a high order to accomplish.

Partnership

The absolute respect and acceptance that you have for each other in no way diminishes the romantic aspects of your love, which in fact "bears all, believes, hopes and tolerates all, and nevermore will end."

Advice

Normally people are attacked at their weakest spot. In your case, however, one will seek to attack a particular strength: your positive way of thinking. Therefore watch out particularly for people and occurrances that are totally unfamiliar to you. One is most apt to stumble over stones one does not know.

51
Thunder

The Person

The mystical attracts you, for it is a part of you. You are considered thoughtful, silent and discreet — which is how you want to be and stay. In spite of the fact that your high creative qualities and your farsightedness would predestine you for leading positions, you prefer to lead a calm, contemplative and withdrawn life.

The Situation

You have no enemies, only the wrong wishes. Accept the fact that someone is standing in your way at this time, and that the matter will have a different outcome that you had hoped for. Everything is happening for your best, and it is not necessary for you to understand it all yet.

Partnership

It is more difficult for the two of you to remain together than it is for you to part, although you see this exactly reversed. Therefore be prepared for a surprise — and for a new way together.

Advice

"The worse things get, the friendlier I will be", should become your motto for the near future. Because the reason for the shocks that you now have to face lies in yourself, not outside of you. And that is why a change of direction must be decided within you.

52
The Silence

The Person

You mostly like what you hear when you listen inside yourself: the knowing silence that can be a void or a lesson, a searching or a finding, meditation or stimulus. Only once in a while do you not enjoy listening all that much: when everyday life has you in its grip and you are forced to share your silence with others.

The Situation

It is not advisable to carry out plans at this time. Let things rest, change your course without making a big fuss about it.

Partnership

Your present hyper-active behavior, which your partner is not used to, reveals uncertainty and tends to infect others. This state is only a momentary impression of your personality structure and does not involve your partnership directly, but that is precisely what you have to explain in order to end the tension.

Advice

Learn to take a broader view of things. At the same time, stop looking down on them.

53
Development

The Person

You have deep admiration for the fascinating order that underlies all things and are developing a special talent for sharing the insights you have gained with others, and thereby increasing them. Material and mental growth only interests you personally insofar as it helps you to be of use to others.

The Situation

Growing means becoming, and that requires time. You know that, but others perhaps do not. Be patient and do not try to force anything. Then things will move along visibly.

Partnership

Without the community in which you and your partner are traditionally active, certain parts of your mutuality would also be lost in your partnership. So it is definitely to your advantage not to think solely of yourself.

Advice

Do not attempt to hack your own path through the undergrowth; you would not reach your goal any sooner, but lose your way instead. Under these particular circumstances your impatience is understandable, but paradoxically it also hinders you.

54
Propriety

The Person

Your presence socially is not without far-reaching effect: your vitality is all-encompassing, direct and unavoidable. When you assume responsibility for a person or a matter one can be sure that you will be able to erect a protective wall with your little finger. But also those people that merely glance your way shyly could become your loyal friends — if you will just beat your wings a bit softer.

The Situation

You have worked thoroughly and precisely according to the principle of being at fault yourself, and have thereby tricked your own lethargy: your subconscious mind has known about a new beginning for a long time, and it also knows that you will now stop grasping at straws, because you have finally discovered the limb above you.

Partnership

Perhaps you gave more than was ever asked for. Talk about this openly.

Advice

How did it begin to end? When you can answer this question for yourself, you will have the answer to your problem.

55
Abundance

The Person

Love, prestige, money, friends. Everything will be given you — provided that you never consider it your personal property or a matter of course. For what can you pour into a cup that is full? Where can the next step take you when you are standing on the summit of a mountain? Do not help yourself with both hands, and always share your good fortune with others.

The Situation

You are at the peak of your success. Don't forget to squint when looking into the sun.

Partnership

You have the ideal partner and yet are unable to recognize and appreciate this. That used to be different. Remember how the two of you began, and learn anew, what love is.

Advice

Do not try to side-step an unusual request that is made of you. With relatively little effort you can now set a lot in motion, and this time it is not of prime importance that you understand all of the correlations.

56
The Traveller

The Person

Your interests and propensities may be as intensive as they will, sooner or later others will take their place, and contrary to the people around you, you are well aware of this. Your whole life consists of wandering, discovering and moving on. The only things unchanged remain your nomadic soul and your loyalty to yourself.

The Situation

You can now reach an important stage of your life, if you do not permit yourself to be swayed from your inner course. Ignore everyone and everything that could influence you in this respect.

Partnership

It would be a lot fairer of you to put a stop to your playing with fire now, besides which, the wind could very easily change direction.

Advice

Whoever stays too long, misses the ending. Devote yourself to the realization of your plans soon, and maintain silence about the ways you intend to use.

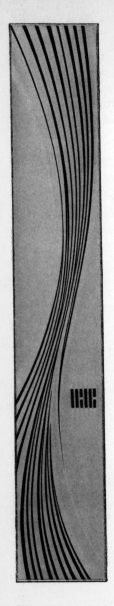

57
Pervasion

The Person

Similar to the branches of a tree that yield to the wind and therefore do not break, your strength lies in gentility, the flexibility of your will. By permitting your adversaries to hold the terrain for awhile, you have ample opportunity to study their strength and methods — and finally you exhaust them with your fearlessness.

The Situation

Your influence increases in proportion to your ability to make credible that your conduct is uniform with that of the others. You will then have the chance to present your true intentions convincingly as well as successfully.

Partnership

Since your love is primarily ruled by your mind, you should not worry your heart with questions now that, naturally, it will not be able to answer. At a later time the situation could certainly reverse itself.

Advice

Do not get involved in anything for which you cannot take responsibility. If necessary, you may have to be prepared to get the work done by yourself.

**58
Joy**

The Person

You can take your pick: your readiness to help makes you an ideal colleague, your motivation an ideal superior, and your generosity an ideal director or manager. Your infectious optimism opens doors and hearts for you.

The Situation

Shortly someone is going to present you with a very pleasant surprise, because you once gave him or her something valuable: courage.

Partnership

You are particularly happy about the contentment in your partnership, the fact that both of you realize how right this relationship is.

Advice

Pay particular attention now to what is said. And to everything you say. Do not let yourself be provoked. Stay friendly in order to remain calm and unassailable.

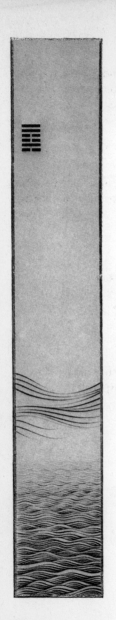

59
Dissolution

The Person

Symbolically you could be depicted as the dove of peace: you turn chaos into order, conflicts into unity, hostility into friendship and tears into laughter. You manage this with quiet selflessness, always following your heart and your intuition.

The Situation

The time is near in which you can devote all of your charitable feelings to a task that is tailored to your inclinations and intentions.

Partnership

Your partner must learn to understand that you are there for all people that need you, and that this will never touch your loyalty to him or her. But you will know how to solve this problem, too.

Advice

Although you are not particularly interested in purely material considerations, it would be unwise for you to spend your money too liberally at this time.

60
The Limitation

The Person

As you are intent on moderation in everything, you consequentially do not make an exception when it comes to your own wishes. So you lead a life limited to essentials and cultivate your affinity for the meditative experience of life.

The Situation

In a matter concerning you someone is waiting for your approval. Retain your healthy skepticism; check the color of the words.

Partnership

Boundaries can not only separate people, they can also bring two sides together.

Advice

You are supposed to believe that your presence is now required elsewhere. You would be ill advised, however, to undertake a trip at this time.

61
Insight

The Person

You have a number of special gifts and therefore corresponding obligations, and you are well aware of them. Your ethical as well as spiritual wealth lies in your conscious commitment to acting according to the principle of cells: multiplication through division. Your sensitivity lets you evaluate people and circumstances in detail and with certainty, and master difficult situations sovereignly. Your ever-present courtesy and your humility come from the heart. You are a person one never forgets.

The Situation

Your capabilities are now being recognized and you will be entrusted with fitting positions. You will learn more about the effect your words can have, and learn to do justice to this responsibility.

Partnership

As long as you keep secrets from your partner and he or she cannot fathom your true motives, there will always be misunderstandngs between the two of you. Have no compunctions about being completely open.

Advice

Stay receptive, like a jug that can only be filled anew when it has permitted itself to be emptied first.

62
The Moderate Excess

The Person

The difficult part about perfection is never knowing where it ends. No wonder that the thought never even occurs to you that you might be carrying something too far! In view of the unchecked exclusiveness, with which you devote yourself to everything, less would sometimes be more.

The Situation

The cup cannot be just a bit too full. You have missed an opportunity to end a matter at the right moment. Do not lose yourself in details now. Instead see to it that the slate is cleaned right away.

Partnership

You need to do nothing except remain yourself. Your partner approves of you much more than you yourself at this time.

Advice

Keep your emotions under control, even the positive ones. Otherwise you will be overrun by a resonance beyond your control.

The Person

You continue to look ahead even when you have reached your goal. For you there is no end, merely a constellation of new and constantly changing beginnings. That makes it easy for you — and you for others — to exit from situations with dignity, to disassociate yourself from tasks, positions, property and personal relationships when the karmic situation demands it.

The Situation

You life will change fundamentally, much to your liking. You will discover new possibilities, interests and goals. Clear up everything that could hinder you, above all a personal problem.

Partnership

You have fought for the peaceful mood now prevalent in your partnership, and you should harmonize the relationship more deeply. Do not permit trivia to be overrated again.

Advice

Even though your patience is being tried: you cannot hurry the changes in store for you. Use the time to prepare yourself for a new set of circumstances in every sense.

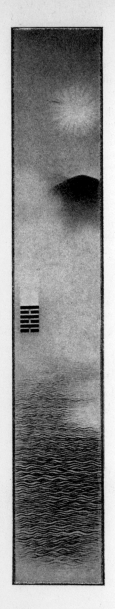

64
Prior to Completion

The Person

With the aid of beginner's luck you are performing a daring high wire dance across the chasms of life. And you are well aware that a mere touch of uncertainty will cost you your balance; a bit too much self-assurance, and you will lose sight of the wire. Therefore it is good for you to consider every step carefully before you take it, to allow yourself time and to be prepared to ward off any attempt at distraction. The goal that you have set for yourself justifies every effort.

The Situation

You believe that you recognize something that is crossing your path. But what you are really seeing is an effect. What you need to find, however, is the cause. What is happening is not a reincarnation of the situation, it is a reincarnation of your yet to be mastered task.

Partnership

You are facing a new phase of your life, and are probably not pondering matters of partnership at the time. But should you be, be aware of and try to accept the fact that the final result of a given process cannot be known before its beginning.

Advice

Make yourself aware in a constructive way that there is a lot yet to discover and to understand. You are sowing still — hopefully you are sowing at all!

Determining a Hexagram-Number

Identify your upper trigram in the horizontal top row and the lower one in the vertical left-hand column. Tracing the respective column down and accross shows you the square at their junction that contains the correct hexagram-number.

The 64 Hexagrams

Upper trigram ▶ / Lower trigram ▼	Qian	Chen	Kan	Ken	Kun	Sun	Li	Dui
Qian	1	34	5	26	11	9	14	43
Chen	25	51	3	27	24	42	21	17
Kan	6	40	29	4	7	59	64	47
Ken	33	62	39	52	15	53	56	31
Kun	12	16	8	23	2	20	35	45
Sun	44	32	48	18	46	57	50	28
Li	13	55	63	22	36	37	30	49
Dui	10	54	60	41	19	61	38	58

Example:
You have arrived at this set of lines: ☰☰
In the horizontal row you find the upper trigram Li and in the vertical column the lower trigram Kun. Their junction is square 35: Progress.

When you apply the knowledge you have gained here, do so the way you would like others to use it in respect to you, or the person you love.

A.H.

Ursula Klinger-Raatz
THE SECRETS OF PRECIOUS
STONES
A Guide to the Activation of the
Seven Human Energy Centers,
Using Gemstones, Crystals and
Minerals
128 Pages
ISBN 0-9415 24-38-8

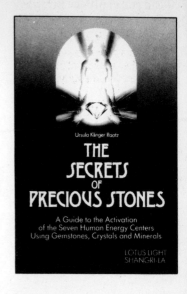

Ursula Klinger Raatz

THE
SECRETS
OF
PRECIOUS STONES

A Guide to the Activation
of the Seven Human Energy Centers
Using Gemstones, Crystals and Minerals

LOTUS LIGHT
SHANGRI-LA

Since time immemorial precious stones and crystals have been mysteriously fascinating for us human beings. Ursula Klinger Raatz describes the effects various stones have on our energy-body, which responds in a number of ways to the colors, qualities and uniqueness of minerals.

The author tells of her experiences with crystals and precious stones, describes the resonance they evoke, and explains how and why they are assigned to the different rainbow-colored energy centers of the human body.

This enables us to determine the healing vibrations of minerals right for us personally and to learn their practical application for the polarization of our energy centers, for healing using precious stones, and for entering into crystal meditation. Equally important, however, are the many impulses given for intuitive work with the secret powers inherent to the mineral world and particularly precious stones and crystals.

Monika Jünemann
ENCHANTING SCENTS
The Secrets of Aroma Therapy.
Fragrant Essences that stimulate,
activate and inspire body, mind
and spirit
128 Pages
ISBN 0-9415 24-36-1

Monika Jünemann

Enchanting Scents

The Secrets of Aroma Therapy
Fragrant essences that stimulate,
activate and inspire
body, mind and spirit.

LOTUS LIGHT
SHANGRI-LA

This book will carry you away to the world of exquisite, enchanting scents. Various fragrances effect our moods, may stimulate and excite us or bring us calmness and harmony, can bewitch and inspire, or even heal. Since ancient times essential oils and incenses have been employed in healing, for seduction and for religious rituals.

Today we are as captivated by the magic of lovely scents and as irresistably captivated by them as ever. The effects that essential oils have can vary greatly. This book particularly treats their subtle influences, but also presents and describes the plants from which they are obtained. *Enchanting Scents* beckons you to enter the realm of sensual experience, to journey into the world of fragrance through essences.

It is an invitation to employ personal, individual scents, to activate body and spirit, and to let your imagination soar. Here is a key that will open your senses to the limitless possibilities of benefitting from fragrances as stimulators, sources of energy and means of healing, or simply to let them broaden the scope of your own perception.